The
Joy of
PILGRIMAGE

With blessings
on your
journeys,
Linda —
Jan Erikson

The
Joy of
PILGRIMAGE

Lori Erickson

Resurrection Press
An Imprint of
CATHOLIC BOOK PUBLISHING CORP.
Totowa • New Jersey

First published in September, 2007 by
Catholic Book Publishing/Resurrection Press
77 West End Road
Totowa, NJ 07512

ISBN 978-1-933066-05-9

Library of Congress Catalog Number: 2007928275

Cover design by Beth DeNapoli

Cover photo by Lori Erickson: Pilgrims arriving at Santiago de Compostela

Interior photos by Lori Erickson and Robert Sessions

Printed in the U.S.A.

1 2 3 4 5 6 7 8 9

For Bob

ACKNOWLEDGMENTS

In writing this book I have relied upon the kindness of friends both old and new. In particular, I am grateful for the assistance of Katherine Johnstone and Francois Gauthron in France; Patricia Wood Winn, Beatriz Marco, and Claudio Buratti Bermudez in Spain; and Bradley Brennan, Hye Su, Kwan-Jo and Jimyee Park in South Korea. Catherine Quehl-Engel was a delightful traveling companion in France. Mary Ethel Emanuel provided support and inspiration.

Most of all, I am grateful to my husband, Bob, whose wisdom has helped shape these journeys and whose love has lit my way.

Contents

Introduction... 9

1. Visions of Mary: Lourdes... 16

2. In the Footsteps of the Saints:
   Santiago de Compostela 31

3. Holy Wandering: Celtic Pilgrimage 48

4. Sacred Lands: Normandy and Bear Butte 67

5. The Pilgrim's Way: Japan and South Korea........... 81

Afterword: Some Final Thoughts
   on Pilgrimage 101

Additional Pilgrimage Sites 106

Introduction

WHAT is a pilgrimage? The best answer I know comes from Martin Buber's *Tales of the Hasidim.* In it Buber recounts the story of a rabbi named Eisik, son of Yekel, who dreamed that he was to go to Prague, where he would find a treasure hidden underneath the bridge leading to the king's palace. At first Eisik dismissed the dream, but after it came to him three more times, he set out on the long journey to Prague.

In the city Eisik found the bridge that had appeared in his dreams, but it was heavily guarded by soldiers. He hung around the bridge, uncertain what to do, until the captain of the guard finally approached him and asked if he was looking for something. Eisik told him of the dream that had brought him to this spot from many miles away. The captain laughed long and hard, and then told him that such dreams were just foolishness. Why, he himself had once had a dream that told him to go to Crakow and dig for treasure under the stove of a Jew named Eisik, son of Yekel. How ridiculous!

You can guess the rest of the story: Rabbi Eisik returned home to Crakow, where he looked under his stove and found the treasure.

The tale illustrates the fact that sometimes we have to travel far to find the riches that are hidden close to us. The impulse to go on such a journey may come in the form of a dream, a chance encounter, or a persistent yearning that refuses to be silenced. Like Eisik, we tell ourselves that we are foolish for listening to that inner voice, and yet we pack our bags and set out. On our journey we may be given insights in forms we don't expect, so that when we return, we find our lives mysteriously enriched.

Virtually all religions recognize the power of pilgrimage. Muslims journey to Mecca, Hindus to the Ganges River, Jews to the Western Wall in Jerusalem, and Christians to the sites connected to the lives of Jesus and the saints. The object of a pilgrimage is not rest and relaxation (though that may happen), but rather spiritual growth. It often begins with questions: Who am I? What is my purpose in life? What do I need to hear? What can draw me closer to God? What do I need to heal my wounds?

The first pilgrim in the Jewish and Christian traditions is Abraham, who leaves his home at God's command to seek a new land. God tells Abraham in Genesis 12:1, "Go from your country and your kindred and your father's house to the land that I will show you. I will make of you a great nation, and I will bless you, and make your name great so that you will be a blessing." The rest of the Old Testament is full of stories of pilgrims, from the Israelites wandering in the desert to the devout who flocked to the city of Jerusalem to worship in the Temple, singing psalms along the way.

For Christians, the scriptural basis of pilgrimage includes Jesus' command to leave home and family and follow him. Throughout two millennia, countless

Christians have gone on pilgrimage, traveling to sites in the Holy Land and to places associated with religious figures, as well as to wild places where they could hear the voice of God more clearly. Pilgrimage came to full flower in the Middle Ages, when everyone from kings to paupers sought inspiration by journeying. Chaucer's *Canterbury Tales* provides a colorful window into the tradition of trips to the English shrine at Canterbury, while John Bunyan's *Pilgrim's Progress* was a popular seventeenth-century allegory of Christian life. Pilgrims would set out for a wide variety of reasons: for adventure, to fulfill a vow, for penance, to strengthen their faith, or to seek healing for themselves or a loved one.

My own interest in pilgrimage began in my childhood, though it would be years before I recognized what kind of seed had been planted. Growing up on an Iowa farm, travel was something that other people did, as remote to my own experience as space exploration. But nearly every Sunday, a different world was revealed to me when we visited my grandparents. While the adults talked I would disappear into a set of musty books called the *John L. Stoddard Lecture Series*. Stoddard was a Victorian adventurer who in the late-nineteenth century traveled the world from Boston to Bombay. Through his words and the sepia-toned photographs that accompanied them, I began to dream of the wonders of faraway places.

My passion for travel led me to become a freelance writer, and in twenty years of writing I have been fortunate to tour some of the same places that Stoddard wrote about in his books. Whether my journey is to a neighboring county or across the globe, I count myself incredibly fortunate to be able to experience other places, cultures, and people. I have also come to believe that travel can be a spiritually transforming experience. I think that is part of what I sensed on those Sunday afternoons spent poring over Stoddard's exotic descriptions and photographs. Travelers exist between worlds and are open to new experiences in ways that don't happen when we are in our familiar routines. Lives and hearts can be changed as a result of what we encounter on the road.

I know my own wanderings have helped shape my spiritual life in unexpected ways. Over the years, I have increasingly found myself drawn to sacred sites on my journeys. Places like the healing shrine at Chimayo in New Mexico, the Native American holy mountain of Bear Butte in South Dakota, and the Celtic Christian landmarks in Ireland are just a few of the places that have exerted a powerful pull on my soul. Something that I saw reflected in the faces of pilgrims at those shrines made me want to deepen my own spiritual journey.

What sets a pilgrimage apart from an ordinary trip? Sometimes it is intention—people set out on a journey that they hope will draw them closer to God. Sometimes it happens without a traveler even being aware of it, and it is only with the benefit of hindsight that it becomes apparent that the journey was in fact a pilgrimage.

Not surprisingly, a pilgrim differs from other kinds of travelers. While those on ordinary journeys typically seek comfort and convenience, pilgrims often endure hardship willingly, for the difficulties can become a way of tempering and strengthening their soul. They may travel to a site with a religious association such as Rome or Lourdes, to a remote and beautiful natural place, or to a place of personal significance (the small village in Mexico where their family traces its roots, for example, or the battlefield their father fought on in Europe). Whatever the destination, it is a journey in quest of spiritual insight and greater self-awareness. A pilgrimage is a journey meant to trigger inner transformation. In this act of devotion, souls are healed and lives changed.

The impulse to go on pilgrimage begins in a variety of ways. The decision may emerge from a long period of restless longing, a sudden inspiration, a life change or personal tragedy, or a chance meeting that turns out to have greater significance. Certain books may find their way into your hands. A casual conversation at the bus stop sets you ruminating on something you haven't thought of in years. The ending of your chemotherapy treatment makes you want to set out on a journey to reflect upon your experiences. A milestone birthday triggers itchy feet and a quest for new meaning in your life.

The natural world may speak to you as well. When the Oglala Sioux visionary Black Elk was ready to go on pilgrimage, even the animals spoke to him. "It is time! It is time!" crows cried as they flew past him, bringing a message that could not be ignored.

Once a traveler is on pilgrimage, it is important to cultivate a spirit of self-reflection, openness, and attention. Without it, a pilgrimage becomes only a vacation, for a true pilgrimage is as much an inner journey as an outward one. The attitude of mindfulness and of acceptance of whatever the day brings is far more essential than any physical possession a pilgrim carries. Two travelers may go on exactly the same journey, and one will have a profoundly life-changing experience while the other complains that the food is bad and the sightseeing disappointing.

I think contemporary Christianity is in great need of rediscovering the power of pilgrimage. Too much of our religious practice is a stolid, static affair. By seeking wild and lonely places, by walking in the footsteps of holy ones who have gone before us, and by mingling with other travelers not afraid to ask hard questions, we connect with something that is untamed and untapped within ourselves. We can relearn the ancient wisdom that recognizes that the simple act of walking can soothe our soul and open our hearts to God. We can connect with other pilgrims on the road, learning from them and teaching in return. We can be reminded that we are part of a much larger story, one that has been going on for thousands of years. Most of all, we can awaken to the sacredness of the present moment, escaping from the routines and habits that hold us captive.

This book will take you on a variety of journeys. Included are descriptions of some of the major Christian pilgrimage sites—Lourdes in France, Santiago de Compostela in Spain, and Iona in Scotland—as well as sites that have become hallowed in more secular ways, such as the D-Day Beaches of Normandy. Chapter Five describes Buddhist holy sites in South Korea and Japan and focuses on the bonds that can link pilgrims despite differences in culture, language, and religion. I hope that through these pages you will begin to glimpse the transformative power of such places and that you will be inspired to plan your own pilgrimage. Such a journey does not require a passport or a great deal of money. A pilgrimage is shaped by prayer and intention, not by the exotic nature of the trip.

The early Celtic Christians, those fearless travelers who would set out on the open sea without oars or rudder so that God alone could guide their journeys, believed that the purpose of pilgrimage was to find their "place of resurrection." The felicitous phrase conveys the fact that certain places speak to us deeply, triggering some mysterious alchemy of growth within us that cannot happen if we refuse the call to become a pilgrim.

Your place of resurrection awaits. May this book help you begin your pilgrim's journey.

1

Visions of Mary
Lourdes

∞∞∞

IT began very simply. On February 11, 1858, a fourteen-year-old French girl was gathering wood with her sister and a friend on the outskirts of a village in the foothills of the Pyrenees Mountains. As they walked, the girl heard a noise like a gust of wind, and looked up to see a woman dressed in white and glowing with light standing in an opening in the rock above her. The woman smiled at the girl, who later said that the lady was the loveliest thing she had ever seen. Over the course of the next five months the woman would appear to the girl seventeen more times, bringing a series of messages that would make Lourdes one of the most famous pilgrimage places in the world and the girl, Bernadette Soubirous, a saint.

Today more than five million people stand before that same rock each year, seeking healing in a place that has become synonymous with miracles. They light candles, march in procession, and drink from the water that flows from the grotto. Most of all they pray, following the example set by the simple peasant girl who was transfixed by a radiant vision of light on that February day.

As I was making plans to visit Lourdes, I was surprised by the number of people who were intrigued by my trip. Everyone had heard of Lourdes, even if they weren't Roman Catholic and didn't know the story of what had happened there in 1858. But they knew that Lourdes was a place of healing, and one by one people gave me tokens to deliver to the shrine. A photograph. A rock. An envelope with a prayer inside. A bit of cloth. Small objects weighted with meaning and hope, many given by people who had a tenuous connection to any kind of religious faith.

After visiting Lourdes, I've come to believe that this place belongs to everyone seeking healing, from the most devout Christian to those who struggle with belief. While Lourdes is a shrine of the Roman Catholic Church, its grotto belongs to all who are sick, brokenhearted, and wounded. Perhaps its most amazing miracle occurs daily and with little fanfare: it happens when the pilgrims who have come here from around the world stand together at the grotto, all differences of culture, status, and wealth erased.

"Everyone who comes to Lourdes is seeking something," I was told by an Irish priest there. While all pilgrims are on a quest, I felt the intensity of that search more strongly in Lourdes than at any other pilgrimage site I have visited.

The young girl who first saw the Virgin Mary that February day in Lourdes was an unlikely visionary. She lived in a mountain village far from the urban and political centers of Europe. Once fairly prosperous, her family's fortunes had declined to the point that they were living in a dank and miserable room that had once been the village jail. She was illiterate and in poor health, having contracted cholera and tuberculosis as a child. The girl worked as a hired servant and spoke only the local dialect. But Bernadette had an inner strength that belied her quiet manner and deprived upbringing: she knew she had experienced something remarkable, and she never wavered in the telling of her story.

The place where she received her visions was known by the villagers as Massabielle, or the old rock. It was hardly a scenic spot, for below the outcropping was a dirty and unkempt area where pigs rooted. The beautiful visions experienced by Bernadette were all the more startling because of the filth that lay just below where the lady appeared.

The first vision was without words. "I saw a young lady dressed in white," Bernadette would later recount. "She wore a white dress, with an equally white veil, a blue belt and a yellow rose on each foot."

Her sister and friend didn't share in the vision, but Bernadette in her excitement couldn't keep her experience to herself. When they returned home, her sister told their mother what had happened. Bernadette was sternly warned not to go to Massabielle again, but an inner force drew her back and Bernadette returned to the spot three days later. Again the lady appeared, and Bernadette prayed the rosary in front of her, as she had done during the first apparition. When Bernadette sprinkled holy water at her, the lady smiled and bent her head.

During the third apparition, the lady spoke for the first time when Bernadette asked her to write her name. "It is not necessary," she replied, then added, "I do not promise to make you happy in this world but in the other. Would you be kind enough to come here for a fortnight?"

Word of the strange events occurring at Massabielle quickly spread. Onlookers began to gather when Bernadette went to the outcropping. While they didn't share in the visions, they could see that Bernadette was transfixed by some mysterious force while standing before the grotto. She was immune to distraction and impervious to pain (once a large pin was even stuck into her shoulder to try to break her trance).

The fortnight requested of Bernadette stretched into five months, with the lady appearing again and again to Bernadette. Disturbed by the growing crowds and worried that the visions were of demonic origin, local civic and church authorities urged Bernadette to confess to lying, but she held firm in her story.

During the ninth apparition, Bernadette astonished the hundreds of people who were present by suddenly falling to her knees and digging in the dirt. The lady had told her to dig, and when she did a spring appeared. A few days later a woman immersed her injured arm in the water and was miraculously healed. Once word of the healing spread, even more people flocked to the grotto.

The lady continued to give Bernadette messages, saying that she wanted people to repent and do penance, and that priests were to build a chapel at the grotto and lead processions there. During the sixteenth apparition, she finally gave Bernadette an answer to the question of her identity: "I am the Immaculate Conception," she said, using a phrase that puzzled the young girl.

By the time of the last vision on July 16, so many people were gathering at the grotto that barriers had been erected to keep the crowds under control. Even Bernadette herself couldn't approach the scene, and so her final vision of the lady was from across the Gave River. The woman was more beautiful than ever, Bernadette said, and she felt as if she was standing right before her instead of across the river.

While the visions had ended, the story of Lourdes was just beginning. After at first distancing themselves from the story, church officials eventually embraced Bernadette's visions, in large part because of the lady's statement that she was the Immaculate Conception. The phrase referred to a theological doctrine that had been declared official church teaching just four years before, the belief that Mary had been conceived without original sin. The uneducated Bernadette didn't know the significance of the phrase, but simply repeated it to her local priest. The statement supported the belief that the Virgin

Mary had indeed chosen to appear in this obscure mountain village.

The fame of the grotto also grew because of the healings that started to happen there. First it was the woman with the injured arm, then a man who regained sight in an eye. As word spread, the sick began to flock to Lourdes from throughout Europe. In an age when medical care was still primitive, many people sought cures from the water that was said to have miraculous properties. The area in front of Massabiele was cleared of rubbish, and in 1871 the Church of the Immaculate Conception was completed. At around the same time the spring uncovered by Bernadette was piped to baths where the sick could immerse themselves and was also sent to fountains where pilgrims could drink and fill containers to take home.

Bernadette's life changed forever as a result of her visions in the grotto. She was sent to the local school, where she learned to read and write. Her fame meant that she was continually pressed to repeat her story. She never altered any significant details, though surely she must have tired of the attention. "I am here to tell you what happened," she would say. "I am not here to make you believe."

In 1866, at the age of twenty-two, Bernadette entered a convent at Nevers, a town 500 miles away. She would never return to the site that had made her name famous. In the convent she worked in the infirmary caring for the sick. She died of tuberculosis at the age of thirty-five, her constitution clearly weakened by the years of poverty and hardship she had endured while young.

In 1933, Bernadette was declared a saint by Pope Pius XI. By that time, Lourdes had become one of the most famous places in the world.

It can be a bit disorienting to visit a site that holds such a large place in the popular imagination. As a friend and I drove into Lourdes on a gray day in February, it seemed like any other small French town (though with far more hotels than comparably sized places). There was even a McDonald's on the main thoroughfare through town.

Once I checked into my hotel and started to walk its streets, however, my first impressions of the town began to change. The closer I came to the shrine, the more unusual Lourdes seemed. Crowds of people began to gather and I heard snatches of conversation in many different languages. Soon I came upon dozens of shops filled with religious gift items: statues, rosaries, jewelry, and crosses. Many also sold containers designed to hold water from the shrine, plastic jugs with the image of the grotto imprinted on them.

Most of all, everywhere I looked I could see the Virgin Mary. Figurines of her filled the open-air shops, her kind visage smiling at passersby. Sometimes her hands were folded in prayer as she gazed upwards to heaven. Other times her hands were outspread in blessing.

   As the entrance to the shrine approached, the crowds got even thicker. I was visiting Lourdes on the days surrounding February 11, the anniversary of the first apparition and a feast day of Bernadette. More than 20,000 pilgrims would join me in the celebrations at the shrine. (About 25,000 pilgrims are present daily in Lourdes during the main pilgrimage season that runs from Easter through the end of October.) The diversity of people was striking: nuns in long habits, elderly couples, young people traveling in groups, elegant Italian women in fur coats, and groups of men holding large banners aloft bearing the names of their cities and churches. As the parade of people passed, I was reminded of the characters in *The Canterbury Tales*, Geoffrey Chaucer's stories about a fourteenth-century pilgrimage to Canterbury, England. He would recognize this air of excitement and anticipation, I thought, though the young people's facial piercings would likely surprise him.

After several more blocks, the commercial district ended and I reached the entrance to the shrine. Just inside St. Joseph's Gate, a large marble statue depicted the Virgin Mary appearing to a man in a hospital bed. A few more steps and a huge basilica came into view, an imposing structure with a gilded crown set atop its lower level. Two ramps extended like arms from each side, ending in a huge square and esplanade capable of holding many thousands of people. Lourdes had clearly changed from the time Bernadette had seen her first vision.

Once I wandered around to the side of the basilica, however, I was relieved to see that the heart of the grotto remained essentially the same as it had been all those years before. The large outcropping of stone known as Massabiele was still there, and in the niche where the lady had appeared to Bernadette stood a statue of the Virgin Mary, her hands joined in prayer as her eyes gazed heavenward. Below, a long line of people slowly wound into the area beneath the stone, where they reverently touched the rock and left photographs, flowers, and other tokens near the spring that had been uncovered by Bernadette. A rack of candles burned brightly in front of the grotto, and nearby was a line of spigots where people collected water from the spring.

While the grotto was the heart of the sanctuary, I found the rest of the complex intriguing as well. Several huge churches welcome the hordes of pilgrims that throng here, each with many services throughout the day and evening. My favorite was the Basilica of Our Lady of the Rosary, a Roman-Byzantine structure with exquisite mosaics. The image of the Virgin Mary above its altar was one of the most beautiful I'd ever seen.

While its physical setting is striking, the shrine's power is also interwoven with the pilgrims who journey here. Scenes from my time there stand out sharp and clear in my memory. I remember a young woman, her face open and vulnerable, kneeling on the cement before the grotto in the falling rain, and a friar wearing a brown cape who looked like he had stepped out of a tapestry from the Middle Ages. I recall the Italian woman who noticed me standing near the water fountains and gestured me forward with a broad smile and the words "Bella! Bella!" I remember the many people in wheelchairs at all the processions and services, and the pilgrims who waited patiently to take their turn in the baths near the grotto.

The words of the Irish priest echoed in my mind: "Everyone who comes to Lourdes is seeking something."

What they seek more than anything is healing, for this place, more than any other pilgrimage spot, is associated with miraculous cures. Sixty-six have been officially documented by the Roman Catholic Church, which maintains a Medical Bureau at the shrine. Cures must meet a stringent set of criteria. Prior to coming to Lourdes, the person must have received a medical diagnosis of an illness regarded as incurable by current means. The cure has to be complete and permanent. The bureau doesn't certify such cures as a miracle—that determination is made by the church—but it does pronounce some cures as "inexplicable."

But the official miracles are only a small subset of the healings that have happened at Lourdes. In order to understand the meaning of this shrine, one must reflect on the difference between curing and healing. A cure is a reversal or an abatement of physical symptoms. The tumor disappears, the paralyzed person stands up and walks. Healing goes deeper. While it may include a physical cure, healing is a restoration of the heart into wholeness. A person may come to Lourdes and receive a dramatic healing of the spirit, then return home to die. Has a miracle occurred? Not one that can be recorded by the Medical Bureau at Lourdes, but most would argue that it is a miracle—a sign of extraordinary grace—nevertheless.

Those seeking physical healing are ever-present at Lourdes. Officials estimate that more than 80,000 sick and disabled pilgrims come to Lourdes each year. More than 100,000 volunteers assist in caring for these people, transporting them from the train station and airport, caring for them in the special accommodations set aside for the sick near the shrine, and helping them as they make their way to services.

Wherever they go, the sick are given pride of place in Lourdes, for this place exists for them most of all.

The obvious question remains: what happens when a pilgrim comes to Lourdes and doesn't receive a healing?

I'm reminded of a story told to me by a friend. A college student had traveled to Lourdes to pray for her mother who was dying of cancer. The young woman went to confession and attended mass. She brought back water from the spring. But after she returned her mother died, and in her bitterness the young woman lost both her mother and her faith.

Lourdes, like all genuine holy sites, is a place of power, and that power can be used for good or ill. It's tempting to think of Lourdes as a magical talisman, a spot where all one has to do is collect some water and say a prayer and all will be well. Life doesn't work like that, of course, even in places where the divine seems very close. It is a mystery why some receive healing at Lourdes and some don't, no matter how deep and genuine their faith.

But what a pilgrimage to Lourdes can do is help us look deeply inside ourselves to find where our wounds are. In the long journey to the shrine we are given time to think and reflect on the state of our lives. This is where I have gone astray. This is where I need healing. And once we arrive, once we are standing shoulder to shoulder with all the other pilgrims who have journeyed from afar, we can feel a kinship that goes deeper than words, and experience a sense of peace that passes understanding.

That wise Irish priest gave me another clue to help understand the mystery of the shrine. "Lourdes is a place of paradox," he told me. "The first paradox is that suffering people come here from all over the world, and yet this is not a place of sadness, but of joy. The second paradox is even greater: in the grotto, light never penetrates, but still a bright light shines forth from it."

On my last day in Lourdes, I thought of that light often. Everywhere around me I could see candles, which are a central part of the pilgrim traditions at the shrine. People buy them to be burned at the grotto as a sign of their prayers and petitions. Candles are also held by pilgrims during the famous evening processions, when thousands of people hold them aloft as they sing hymns of praise. The ribbons of flickering light winding through the darkness are an apt metaphor for the beacon of hope that Lourdes provides to the world. Even on those gray February days of my visit, that light shone brightly in the faces of the pilgrims I met at Lourdes.

It is not surprising, I think, that so many of the great pilgrimage sites are connected with the Virgin Mary, from Fatima in Portugal to the shrine of Our Lady of Guadalupe in Mexico City. These sites have a special place in the hearts of pilgrims because of the nurturing mother who stands at the center of them. Like any mother, she beckons her children to come home, an invitation that is answered by millions of people each year.

As for me, when I recall my trip to Lourdes I remember the grand drama of my experiences there, the processions and masses and the exultant feeling of being surrounded by so many pilgrims. But I recall with special fondness something that may seem small and trivial in comparison—all those shops selling Virgin Mary souvenirs. While one can complain about the commercialism, I think there's something pleasingly subversive about those endless shelves of knick-knacks. I imagine the places where those trinkets are likely to end up, how they will find their way into nursing homes, hospital rooms and bedside tables, into the pockets of chemotherapy patients and the hands of soldiers going off to war. Though small and inexpensive, those tokens carry a powerful message: they are a reminder that the broken and wounded will be the first to enter the Kingdom of God, that miracles are possible even when the darkness seems overwhelming, and that the most unlikely among us can receive a life-changing vision of light.

When I returned home from Lourdes, I took great joy in handing out the things I had purchased. "This is for you," I would say as I delivered each one. "From Mary."

And in the responses of friends—even those who struggled with belief—I saw something familiar. I recognized the light in their eyes, because I had already seen it on the faces of the pilgrims in the grotto.

2

In the Footsteps of the Saints
Santiago de Compostela

IN the middle of a large public square in the Spanish city of Santiago de Compostela lies a paving stone engraved with the image of a shell and these simple words: Camino de Santiago. For hundreds of years pilgrims have stood on this spot, gazing at the imposing, twelfth-century cathedral that rises before them. Those who gather here are often footsore and weary after weeks of journeying across plains and mountains. Many have made this journey to deepen their faith or fulfill a vow, others to perform a penance, and some out of a sense of adventure. All end their wanderings here, before the church where the remains of the apostle St. James (Santiago in Spanish) are said to lie. After more than a thousand years, the Camino de Santiago—the Way of St. James—continues to inspire Christians from around the world.

In an era in which it's easy to step onto a plane and be deposited nearly anywhere in the world, the Way of St. James is a reminder of the power of pilgrimages taken slowly and deliberately. The path to Santiago de Compostela is meant to be walked, for the journey is as important as actually standing at the crypt of the apostle. Once all pilgrimages were like this, journeys that took weeks or months of hard travel. But of the three most famous Christian pilgrimages—to Jerusalem, Rome, and Santiago de Compostela—only the Way of St. James has remained a route that many pilgrims take on foot.

A confession: when I visited Santiago, I did not walk the full route into the city. But I hiked enough of the Way of St. James to begin to appreciate the immense age and evocative appeal of this storied route. As I traveled through Galicia, the region of Spain in which the shrine is located, I fell in love with its misty, melancholy beauties. In many ways this green and mountainous land has more in common with Ireland than with the sun-baked plains of La Mancha. After touring its byways, I arrived in Santiago de Compostela with insights into what the journey means to pilgrims of all denominations. Galicia is a magical place, and it is no surprise that travelers have been falling under its spell for more than a millennium.

The story of the pilgrimage to Santiago de Compostela is intertwined with the history of Christianity. After Jesus' resurrection, St. James became the leader of the church in Jerusalem. According to tradition, he also traveled to Spain to spread the Good News, then returned to Jerusalem where he was martyred. Following his death, his followers are said to have taken his body to the coast, where a ship was miraculously waiting for them. The body of St. James was interred in a tomb in north-western Spain, after which its location fell into oblivion for centuries.

Around the year 815, a Spanish hermit named Pelayo had a vision in which he saw a bright light shining over a spot in a forest. The matter was investigated and a Roman-era tomb containing St. James' body was found. The bishop of a nearby town, Theodomir, had a church built on the site of the tomb. Around this shrine the city of Santiago de Compostela grew (while its origins are not certain, Compostela may come from the Latin *campus stellae*, "field of stars"). The shrine began attracting pilgrims, who steadily increased in number until by the eleventh and twelfth centuries, a half-million pilgrims a year were making their way to Santiago.

The pilgrimage drew the devout from across Europe for several reasons. In the year 1122 Pope Calixtus II granted the city various privileges, including an indulgence for those who journeyed here on pilgrimage, with special consideration given to those who made the pilgrimage in a year when the Feast of St. James (July 25) fell on a Sunday. Spanish Bishop Diego Gelmirez was a strong advocate for the city as well, starting a large-scale building program that included the construction of its immense Romanesque cathedral, as well as facilities for the many pilgrims who made their way to Santiago. The kings of the neighboring lands of Aragon, Navarre and Castile contributed to the route's popularity by building bridges, hospitals, and other pilgrim services, often entrusting the work to the monks of the French order of

Cluny. While many roads led to Santiago from all over Europe, the most traveled became the French Road, which passes over the Pyrenees Mountains before entering Galicia.

The Way of St. James was difficult, but for many pilgrims it offered a much easier trip than the journey to Jerusalem or Rome. Monuments, churches, monasteries, towns, and cities grew up along the network of roads leading to Santiago, and the city itself benefited greatly from the spiritual, economic and cultural growth stimulated by the millions of pilgrims. The Way of St. James became the first great thoroughfare of Christian Europe, a meeting place for people from a wide variety of backgrounds and nations. On the road pilgrims from many countries mingled, from Amsterdam and Gdansk to Lisbon and Zagreb.

As the route grew in popularity, so did the legends and lore associated with it. The scallop shell became the symbol of the pilgrimage, in part because the shells were common along the Atlantic beaches just west of Santiago. Travelers would wear a scallop shell to proclaim their status as pilgrims, and the motif was incorporated into many of the buildings, wells, churches, and monuments along the route. The shell was also the subject of a legend that said that when the body of St. James was being returned to Spain, a knight fell from a cliff on shore and drowned as the body passed by. When the knight miraculously arose alive from the water, he was covered in scallop shells.

Because of the popularity of the pilgrimage, Santiago de Compostela became the spiritual capital of Spain and St. James the nation's patron saint. In iconography and statues the apostle was frequently pictured wearing the pilgrim's hat and cloak, carrying a staff and water gourd. Another common way of picturing the apostle was as a knight mounted on horseback.

For many centuries, the pilgrimage drew both the wealthy and the poor. A pilgrimage was seen as an enactment of the spiritual journey to Christ, and the hardships along the way were welcomed as tests of faith.

In the seventeenth century, Sir Walter Raleigh immortalized the pilgrimage with words that remain popular among pilgrims to this day:

> *Give me my scallop shell of quiet;*
> *My staff of faith to walk upon;*
> *My scrip of joy, immortal diet;*
> *My bottle of salvation;*
> *My gown of glory, hope's true gauge*
> *And then I'll take my pilgrimage.*

While the Way of St. James declined in popularity following the Middle Ages, the past five decades have seen a steady growth in the number of pilgrims. Today an estimated 40,000 travelers make the journey each year, many traveling for religious reasons, others because of the way's status as one of the great cultural routes of Europe. (In 1987 UNESCO designated the Way of St. James as the first European cultural itinerary, and the city of Santiago de Compostela itself is a World Heritage Site.)

The appeal of the Way of St. James is linked to the unique character of Galicia, a region of deep forests, dramatic gorges and canyons, and many rivers. Along with Ireland, Scotland, Wales, Cornwall, Isle of Man, and Brittany in France, Galicia is considered one of the seven Celtic nations. The Celts came here in the fifth century B.C.E., leaving behind a treasure trove of dolmens (slabs of rocks arranged in table form), petroglyphs, and fortified hamlets of stone, as well as Galician bagpipes and an abiding love for fantasy and myth. To this day the intensely green and rugged landscape of Galicia, often wreathed in mist and rain, shares a common heritage and ethos with the other Celtic lands.

The history of Galicia was also influenced by the Romans, who considered this region to be the end of the world, or *Finis Terrae* in Latin. It was believed that the sun died each evening off its rocky coast, and that from this point the souls of the dead embarked for the next life.

Because of its location on the western coast of Europe, the Galician character owes more to the stormy Atlantic than to the sunny Mediterranean. Even today the Galicians are said to be more melancholic than their fellow Spaniards, in part because in this historically poor region, many have had to emigrate to other lands to survive. Those who stayed often lived in isolated villages where the old ways and traditions remained strong.

The gift that such isolation and hardship brought was a deepening of the Galician soul. One can sense that, I think, on travels through this moody and haunted place. It's not surprising that the miraculous story of the relics of St. James would gain such widespread devotion here. Far from the centers of power in Europe, Santiago de Compostela—and the sites along the Way to St. James—gained spiritual stature instead.

The Way of St. James, then, includes far more than the relics that lie at the end of the route. It is a thousand memorable sites along the way, in tiny villages with centuries-old stone cottages, by the side of sacred springs gushing from deep within the earth, down well-worn footpaths that wind through dark forests, and in magnificent monasteries built to house the endless stream of pilgrims who traveled along the routes that converge on Santiago.

While a description of the landmarks along the Way of St. James could easily fill many books, I have my own favorites. In my mind's eye I can picture how the rain fell softly amid the statuary in the cloisters in the Benedictine monastery at Samos, one of the largest monasteries in Spain. I remember visiting a convent in the city of Tui, where a cloistered nun sold us rosaries through a grille window, her face barely visible. As we walked away, our guide—his normal cynicism uncharacteristically absent—wondered aloud who would pray for the city once the elderly nuns living inside had died.

For me and for many pilgrims, one of the most memorable spots is the humble village of O Cebreiro, which sits near the top of a mountain near the eastern border of Galicia. For centuries travelers have reached this high refuge by hiking up the mountain through the mist, guided by the sound of the bells ringing from the small village church. The church is a beloved landmark in Galicia because of a Eucharistic miracle that took place here in the fourteenth century. As my tour group stood before its altar, our guide told us the story, in which an apostate priest regained his lost faith when the wine he was consecrating turned to blood in the chalice (the vessel is featured on the Galician coat of arms). "This church is one of the most famous along the entire Way of St. James," he said. "You are standing where many pilgrims have stood before you, including St. Francis."

At that moment in the quiet country church high in the mountains of Spain, the years fell away and I felt the connection that links all pilgrims along this ancient route. Those who seek the blessing of Santiago de Compostela travel not only in space but also in time, linked in some mysterious way to all the saints and sinners who have gone before them. For a brief time it was not hard to imagine St. Francis standing beside me, our eyes gazing upwards at the chalice before us.

Before we left the church, our guide pointed out another treasure, the statue of Santa Maria la Real, the patron saint of the village. He said that the statue leans forward from the wall because at the moment when the wine became blood, Mary tilted her head forward so she could better contemplate the miracle.

Another place that haunts my memories of Galicia is the deep canyon known as the Ribeira Sacra, or sacred bank. Formed by the rushing waters of the River Sil, this wild and rugged region is known both for its wines (called the "wines of heaven" because they come from grapes grown on impossibly steep slopes) and for its spiritual heritage. A thousand years ago, the canyon became a sanctuary for monks and hermits, who built at least twenty monasteries, grottos, and churches here. The Ribeira Sacra is said to contain the greatest concentration of monasteries in Europe after Greece. In this isolated spot, Christians sought to escape the temptations of the world by following the example of the Desert Fathers and Mothers who had fled to the Egyptian desert in the third and fourth centuries.

The remains of a number of Romanesque structures can be found here. The most dramatic spot is San Pedro de Rocas, or St. Peter on the Rock. Dating back to the sixth century, it was one of the first monastic dwellings in Spain and is located next to a spring that was likely considered holy long before Christianity arrived in Europe.

Carved out of the rocky side of the mountain, the structure's grotto-like interior is hushed and dark, a place that invites introspection and prayer. Outside, a path leads to the sacred spring surrounded by mossy boulders. Its waters are said to bring healing to the devout who journey here.

A few miles away, the Santa Cristina Monastery provided another tranquil spot for reflection. The ruins of the church, situated in an ancient chestnut forest, cling to the side of the canyon and overlook the river far below. Sitting within the broken-down walls of its cloister, I remembered a Japanese term that I had never fully understood before: *wabi-sabi*, which is used to describe the loveliness to be found in things that are imperfect, impermanent, and incomplete. Sitting in that serene enclosure, I began to have a sense for the meaning of that perspective, which is so different from our Western notion that beauty is best expressed in that which is perfect. *Wabi-sabi* recognizes instead that everything that lives will eventually die, and in the decay there can be a profound beauty.

Places like this ruined monastery invite reflection. In order to find such spots, we must seek out hidden places far from the crowds that often throng holy places. We must be willing to sit and do nothing, to listen and be silent, so that the spirit of the place can speak to us. In that lonely spot in a place long abandoned by the rest of the world, Santa Cristina spoke to me of the inevitable passage of time and of my own mortality: no small gift to receive while on pilgrimage.

Whatever route one takes to Santiago, the end of the journey is the same today as it has been for a thousand years: the cathedral of Santiago de Compostela, where the relics of St. James are kept. Pilgrims complete their long journey in the huge square that lies before the church, gazing upward at the massive structure formed of Galician granite.

What happens next has, over the centuries, become a highly ritualized set of actions. After climbing the cathedral stairs and entering its doors, the first sight that greets pilgrims is the spectacular *Portico de la Gloria*, an entryway of carved stone that is considered one of the masterpieces of medieval art. The entryway was created over a twenty-year period by the master sculptor Mateo, who finished the remarkable frieze in 1188. Carved into its center column is the figure of St. James, while above him Christ sits surrounded by his disciples and dozens of other religious figures and motifs, a work one could easily spend a day contemplating (indeed, in the Middle Ages such works were said to be the Bible of the poor).

Pilgrims are instructed to place their hand on the pillar where St. James stands, finding the deep grooves formed by the hands of the millions of travelers who have come here before them. As they touch the pillar, they are to say the prayer of petition that has brought them on pilgrimage. Then they walk to the other side of the column where a small statue stands, a figure that is believed to be the self-portrait of the stonemason Mateo. To receive some of the master's wisdom, they must knock their forehead three times gently on his head.

And then, at last, one can contemplate the interior of the cathedral. At the end of the long center aisle, a dazzling Baroque altar blazes with gold. It includes three depictions of St. James: as teacher, pilgrim, and knight. But this magnificent, overwhelmingly ornate altar welcomes pilgrims in a surprisingly intimate way: visitors are invited to climb the stairs that lead to an area behind the altar, where they can embrace the gilded statue of St. James from behind, wrapping their arms around him in a hug. After this familial embrace, pilgrims descend into the crypt where the saint's relics are kept in a silver casket. The final pilgrim's task is to attend a mass in the cathedral.

If pilgrims are fortunate, they can time their visit to coincide with a service during which the cathedral's *botafumeiro*, a huge incensory made of silver-plated brass, is used. During special services at the cathedral, the 170-pound censer swings like an enormous pendulum through the sanctuary, leaving behind a trail of smoke and the fragrance of incense.

In this hushed sanctuary, an air of holiness is palpable. The cathedral seems filled with the petitions of the millions of pilgrims who have journeyed here over the centuries, bringing their prayers, hopes, dreams, and pleadings for mercy. After traveling so far to arrive here, many people spend hours in contemplation in the church, clearly reluctant to end their pilgrimage.

Outside, more treasures await in Santiago itself. This medieval city of narrow streets and beautiful open squares is made for strolling, particularly in the Old Quarter with its tiny shops, ancient bookstores, and cozy bars. The frequent rain doesn't dampen the mood of the pilgrims, tourists, and university students who fill its busy streets. Dozens of churches, monasteries, museums, and other landmarks surround the cathedral, including the Monastery of St. Martin Pinario, Convent of San Paio, and the Pilgrimage Museum dedicated to telling the story of the Way of St. James.

My time in Santiago de Compostela ended, appropriately enough, in a church—not the grand cathedral where the saint's relics reside, but instead in a nearby convent, where the nuns welcome visitors at the evening mass. As the church grew darker with the fading of the evening light, the nuns began to sing, their voices sounding unearthly, almost silvery in tone. Overwhelmed by the beauty, I could only sit and marvel at how blessed I felt to be one of the many pilgrims who have made their way to Santiago de Compostela.

Travelers hoping to make a pilgrimage along the Way of St. James should note that the number of pilgrims grows dramatically during Jubilee or Holy Years, when more than 100,000 pilgrims make the journey to Santiago. (The next jubilee will come in 2010.) A plenary indulgence is granted to those who make the pilgrimage during these years. During this period, pilgrims enter the cathedral through the Holy Door, which is located behind the altar.

Of the six main routes that lead to the city, the most popular is the French Way, which crosses the Pyrenees Mountains from France into Spain. Other routes include the Northern Way (which travels through the Basque region of Spain) and the Portuguese Way from the south. Many hostels cater to pilgrims traveling by foot, bicycle, or horseback, most charging minimal fees. On the French Way, the distance from the French border to Santiago is approximately 500 miles, a journey that takes about six weeks by foot. About half the route passes over rough terrain, and pilgrims need to be physically fit. The best times to travel are June and September. Many pilgrims also take the route during July and August, but the heat can be oppressive. Travel is not recommended in winter because of frequent rain and occasional snow.

Pilgrims may apply to obtain *La Compostela*, a Latin document issued by the cathedral of Santiago. It is granted to those who travel the way for religious reasons, and is stamped at various points along the route. Walkers must travel at least the last 100 kilometers (about 62 miles), and bicyclists the last 200 kilometers, in order to receive a certificate confirming that they have made the pilgrimage.

Even if one can't make the long journey to Santiago de Compostela, I believe all pilgrims can learn from the Way of St. James. Its most important lesson is that a pilgrimage is as much about the journey as it is about arriving at the destination. Though it is deeply meaningful to stand in the cathedral in Santiago, time spent en route to the shrine is perhaps the more important part of the pilgrimage.

We can take that lesson to heart in our own journeys. Something changes when we walk to our destination rather than drive or fly. It's often not physically possible to do the entire journey by foot, of course, but virtually any journey is improved by walking at least part of the way. By slowing down we force ourselves to contemplate things more deeply and we become more open to our fellow pil-

grims along the way. We have time for prayer and contemplation, moments that are often lost when we travel too quickly.

In my own journeys, I can think of many times when an ordinary trip became sacred in part because I took the time to stop and travel more slowly. This is one reason why backpacking in nature can be such a meaningful experience. Instead of rushing by at 60 miles per hour, we have the time to stop, to reflect, to absorb. We travel mindfully, not mindlessly, honoring the holiness of the journey with each step. And because we must carry what we need on our backs, we are forced to consider what is most essential to us and what can be left behind.

When we do so, even the most ordinary route can be transformed. When Alan Scarfe, Episcopal bishop of Iowa, decided to go on pilgrimage two years ago, he didn't travel to some famed holy place, but rather resolved to walk and run the distance between the two cathedrals in his state. He mapped a 175-mile, nine-day journey between Davenport and Des Moines, a route that took him on busy city streets, deserted country roads, and quiet small town avenues. He invited parishioners from churches along the way to join him as he walked, so that sometimes he was by himself and sometimes with other people.

"I had driven the route by car, but something changed when I did it slowly," he recalls. "Looking back, a number of things stand out to me about the experience. One was the way it brought to life the Biblical passages that speak of Jesus walking with his disciples by the side of the road. I felt a wonderful sense of connection to that part of Jesus' life, something I had never thought much about before."

By the eighth day, Scarfe felt a deepening of his inner life similar to what he has experienced after a multi-day silent retreat. Even though he had been in conversation with others for much of the route, his time spent walking and running such a long distance, often in prayer, had a deep impact on his spiritual life.

"An added benefit was that I ended the pilgrimage with an abiding sense of connection to the countryside of Iowa," he concludes. "Now when I drive by on the interstate and see the exits for those small towns, I remember what it was like to walk through them. I think I have a better understanding of how the land has shaped the people who live here and who worship in our churches."

I invite you to think of places where you might make a walking pilgrimage, even if you can't make the journey to Santiago de Compostela. Walk the route your grandfather took to school each day while growing up, or retrace your own childhood rambles. Follow the path taken by Martin Luther King, Jr., as he led the march in Selma, or trace part of the Trail of Tears taken by the Cherokee in the 1830s. Walk in the footsteps of Thomas Merton at the Abbey of Gethsemani in Kentucky, or hike part of the Appalachian Trail. Wherever you go, travel as a pilgrim, with observant eyes and an open heart, keeping in mind the words of St. Augustine: *Solvitur ambulando*. It is solved by walking.

3

Holy Wandering
Celtic Pilgrimage

A NUMBER of years ago, my husband and I found ourselves on a somewhat unlikely pilgrimage when we lived for five months in the Yorkshire Dales of northern England. It was unlikely in that we didn't even realize until halfway through our time there that we were on a spiritual journey. But the longer we stayed, the more we found ourselves drawn to the many holy sites scattered across Great Britain and Ireland. Some of these sites were pre-Christian in origin: standing stones, dolmens, and passage graves that date back thousands of years before the coming of Christianity. Others were associated with the rich flowering of Christianity that took place in the British Isles between the sixth and eleventh centuries. Places like Iona in Scotland, Glendalough in Ireland, and Lindisfarne in England were deeply moving to us both.

In the years since then, I have come to have even greater respect for the richness of early Celtic Christianity. I'm not alone in my appreciation for this intriguing chapter of Christian history, for Celtic spirituality is being rediscovered by growing numbers of seekers today. It is especially appropriate to talk about these traditions in a book on pilgrimage, for the theme of holy wandering is a central part of Celtic Christianity.

First, some history. During the period when much of mainland Europe was devastated by invasions, war, and the collapse of the Roman Empire, Christianity flourished in the parts of Britain where Celtic peoples lived. Monasteries became centers for learning and spirituality, beacons of civilization in a dark age.

Ireland in particular experienced a period of extraordinary cultural, artistic, and religious growth. Living on the edge of the known world and spared Roman invasion, Irish Christians embraced the Christianity brought to them by St. Patrick and other missionaries, forging a vibrant and creative spirituality that attracted followers from throughout Europe.

Celtic Christianity had a number of distinctive features. Its hallmarks included a deep love for nature, an emphasis on the constant presence of God, and an artistic renaissance that included beautiful illuminated manuscripts, carved High Crosses, and lyrical prayers and hymns. The *Book of Kells*, a lavishly illustrated version of the Gospels now at Trinity College in Dublin, is regarded as one of the most exquisite pieces of religious art in the world.

Among its defining characteristics was a sense that even the simplest and most commonplace of human actions should be invested with ritual and prayer. During the nineteenth century Alexander Carmichael collected many of these traditional oral Celtic prayers in his *Carmina Gadelica.* The compendium is full of invocations for such seemingly mundane activities as greeting the rising sun, covering the fire at night, and getting ready for sleep. This prayer, for example, called upon angels and saints to help with the tending of cattle:

Come, Brendan, from the ocean,
Come, Ternan, most potent of men,
Come, Michael valiant, down
And propitiate to me the cow of my joy.
  Ho my heifer, ho heifer of my love,
  Ho my heifer, ho heifer of my love.
  My beloved heifer, choice cow of every shieling,
  For the sake of the High King take to thy calf.

The Celts understood pilgrimage in a different way than what would later become common. Throughout history most Christians have typically viewed pilgrimage as a journey taken to a particular holy place such as Lourdes, Santiago de Compostela, or Rome. Pilgrims would make the journey and then return to their regular lives.

In Ireland and elsewhere in Britain, a different understanding emerged. Here pilgrimage was seen as the central metaphor for what it means to be a Christian. All Christian life is a journey to God. We live in perpetual exile, constantly seeking after Christ, and our outward journeys are to reflect our inner transformation.

Part of the fondness for journeying was no doubt related to the perpetual Celtic wanderlust. The Celts were a traveling people, and their legends are full of stories of people setting out on a journey after hearing a mysterious call. But the Celtic Christian emphasis on pilgrimage went deeper. In exiling themselves from the comforts of home, pilgrims taught themselves to rely only on God. Celtic Christians had a strong sense that this world was not their true home. They were to be *hospites mundi*, or guests of the world, living lightly on this earth and not becoming attached to possessions or to one location.

Celtic pilgrimage was also often undertaken as a penance. One famous example is the legend associated with the founding of the Christian settlement of Iona off the coast of western Scotland. After the monk Columba was involved in a dispute in his native Ireland, he was banished from his home and took to the sea. Upon reaching Iona, he stood on its highest point and looked back to see if Ireland was still in view. When he couldn't see its shore, he knew that he had fulfilled his penance and could stay and build a new community there. The hill where he looked across the sea is known to this day as *Carn Cuil ri Eirinn*, the "Cairn of him who turned his back on Ireland."

Even if a pilgrimage was not undertaken as a penance, Celtic Christians often sought out desolate and isolated places. In this they drew inspiration not only from Jesus, who often retreated into the wilderness to pray, but also from the Desert Fathers and Mothers of the third and fourth centuries, who left the luxuries of civilization to live in solitude and hardship. Even today you can find hundreds of place names in the British Isles and Ireland that are variations of the word *desert*, including Dysserth, Diseart, and Dysart.

Since misty Ireland is sorely lacking in real deserts, pilgrims would also set off to find (in the words of one early text) the "desert in the ocean." Some would launch themselves in small coracles without oars or maps, trusting themselves entirely to God. Ian Bradley, writing in his book *The Celtic Way*, recounts the story of three monks who set off in a tiny boat without oars or adequate provisions. After seven days the vessel washed up on the coast of Cornwall, where the monks were brought before King Alfred. When he asked them why they had undertaken such a foolish journey, they replied innocently, "We stole away because we wanted for the love of God to be on pilgrimage, we cared not where."

The Celts had a lovely saying for those setting out on pilgrimage: "Let your feet follow your heart until you find your place of resurrection." This was a spot where God's will for their lives would be revealed and fulfilled. The place of their resurrection need not be a famous holy site, and it was unique for each individual. It could be a simple stone hut, a windswept island, or a secluded valley. Certain sites were said to be "thin places," where the veils between worlds was most transparent.

The golden age of Celtic Christianity began to fade, alas, with the start of Viking raids at the end of the eighth century. Over the next centuries many monasteries were repeatedly sacked, their treasures stolen and inhabitants killed. The legacy of Celtic Christianity would be largely forgotten for many years.

Today Celtic Christianity is being rediscovered by a new generation of seekers. Many contemporary prayers, hymns, and meditations draw inspiration from the Celtic tradition. The Celtic practice of *anamchara*, or soul friends who encourage each other on their spiritual journeys, is also enjoying renewed interest. Authors J. Philip Newell and David Adam are among those who are helping to revive interest in Celtic ways of spirituality.

Given this revival of interest, it's not surprising that increasing numbers of pilgrims are traveling to the holy sites of the British Isles. Of all the sites connected with this tradition, the island of Iona off the western coast of Scotland is the best known. When I visited several years ago, I remember thinking that the island seemed impossibly small to bear such a heavy weight of history. Just three miles long and one mile wide, the windswept, rocky island is part of the Inner Hebrides. Pilgrims must first take a ferry to the island of Mull, then travel a winding, narrow road across the length of that island, and finally board another ferry to Iona. You have to want to get to Iona.

As described above, the Irish monk Columba (also known as Columcille) founded the monastic community of Iona in 563. Building a monastery on the site of an old

Druid temple, Columba was a devout and charismatic religious leader. Under his guidance, Iona became a missionary center and the head of a family of monasteries scattered throughout Ireland, Scotland, and northern England. At its height, about 150 monks lived on Iona, making it a center for culture and learning famous throughout Europe. The *Book of Kells* was likely created here during the eighth century, as well as magnificent High Crosses that remain to this day.

In a pattern that would be repeated at many other monastic settlements, Viking raids began around 800 and devastated the community. Several centuries later, Benedictine monks came to Iona to establish a new monastery, building an abbey that still dominates the island. Iona settled into obscurity once again, many of its buildings in ruins.

The island was rediscovered in the Victorian age, when travelers began to recognize the importance of the early Christian settlements here. Sir Walter Scott, John Keats, Felix Mendelssohn, and William Wordsworth all visited the remote island, and scholars began a systematic attempt to study and preserve the ruins.

The modern revival of Iona dates to 1938, when George MacLeod founded the ecumenical Iona Community. The group spearheaded the restoration of the monastic buildings and established a resident community on Iona. The Iona Community has a long-standing interest in liturgical renewal, and its prayers, hymns and songs have been reprinted widely, playing a major role in the revival of interest in Celtic spirituality. The community maintains an active presence on Iona, leading regular worship services and retreat programs.

About a hundred people live on Iona year round, and an additional 150,000 visit the island each year. Its oldest remaining building is St. Oran's Chapel, dedicated to a cousin of Columba. It was built during the twelfth century, though the surrounding burial ground likely dates back to the earliest years of Christian settlement here. Legend says that many of the first kings of Scotland, Ireland, and Norway were buried here, including MacBeth of Shakespearean fame.

While the physical landscape of Iona is dominated by the medieval-era abbey built by the Benedictines, its spiritual landscape is infused with memories of Columba. Thanks to a *Life of Columba* written about 700, we know a considerable amount about this gentle, holy man and the places he loved on the island. The areas where he retreated for prayer and meditation continue to draw pilgrims today.

Iona is a place haunted by history and infused with holiness. Despite being so small, its landscape is surprisingly varied, with white sandy beaches, rolling heather moorland, rocky promontories, sand dunes, and valleys of grass. Pilgrims come here to hear the wild Atlantic surf break against the rocks, to smell the fresh salt air, and to ponder the courage of the Irish monks who set forth in their small boats on the sea, trusting only in God to guide them.

No description of Celtic Christianity would be complete, of course, without mentioning St. Patrick, the patron saint of Ireland. Patrick was likely born in the southwest of England to a Roman-Britain family. At sixteen he was captured by raiders and sold into slavery in Ireland. His master made him work as a shepherd, and so Patrick lived a life of loneliness and isolation as he wandered the green hills of Ireland. That desert experience—for surely it was a desert of the heart despite the frequent rains he no doubt experienced—shaped and tempered the young man's soul. Cut off from his family, unable to speak the native language, Patrick turned more and more to prayer.

After six long years Patrick heard a voice telling him to leave his master and walk to the sea. At the shore he found a boat and persuaded its captain to allow him to join his crew. Patrick eventually returned to his family, becoming a priest and then a bishop in England.

And then Patrick did something that seems totally surprising: in the year 432 he went back to Ireland, back to the place where he had been enslaved and where he had suffered great loneliness and hardship. Once again it was an inner voice that directed his steps, a voice that called him to preach to the Irish.

Preach he did. Largely through the efforts of Patrick, an entire country was converted without violence or coercion. Part of his success lay in his respect for the native holy traditions of the Celts. If a well or high hill was considered sacred to them, Patrick simply

Christianized it. Thus today you can still find countless holy sites in Ireland that blend Christianity with much older traditions, places like Croagh Patrick, a mountain once sacred to the Celtic god Lugh and later a place of Christian pilgrimage.

Like the early apostles, Patrick traveled with few material possessions, relying on the hospitality of those he met. For thirty years he wandered among the native tribes of Ireland, telling everyone he met the story of Jesus. At his death in 461, the Irish mourned him as one of their own.

St. Patrick's legacy is visible throughout Ireland, particularly in the counties of Northern Ireland. Downpatrick, whose name pays homage to the saint, is a good place to begin a Patrick-related pilgrimage. Many sites here celebrate the missionary, including the new Saint

Patrick Centre, a museum that is a focus of studies relating to the patron saint of Ireland. The site tells the story of Patrick through multimedia technology, including scenes from Patrick's life, excerpts from his writings, and exhibits that explore his life and legacy.

After leaving the museum, pilgrims can visit the Cathedral of Down, a medieval Benedictine abbey reworked in the eighteenth century. When Patrick died it is said that oxen carried his body back to that part of Ireland he loved best, and his body was interred here on this hill that overlooks Downpatrick. In fulfillment of an ancient prophecy that foretold three saints would share this most hallowed ground, the bones of St. Columba and St. Bridget are also said to be buried here, making it one of the most important pilgrimage sites in Ireland for more than a thousand years.

The nearby village of Saul contains more memories of Patrick. An exquisite little church stands on the site where Patrick is said to have preached his first church service. Inside are a few pews and a lovely stained glass window depicting the saint, while an ancient graveyard sleeps outside. On a neighboring hill known as Slieve Patrick stands a massive statue of the saint, dedicated in 1933. The spot offers an expansive view of the pastoral, rolling countryside of County Down.

Finally, travelers should visit the Struell Wells, a set of holy wells located in a serene, rural valley two miles east of Downpatrick. Locals say that these were the first springs to be blessed by St. Patrick, and the waters are thought to have the ability to heal both body and spirit.

Countless other sites in Ireland claim an association with St. Patrick as well. One of the most famous is the aforementioned Croagh Patrick in County Mayo, the spot where Patrick is said to have driven the snakes from Ireland. Patrick fasted for forty days on the mountain's summit in 441, and for many centuries it has been a popular pilgrimage site. During the years when penal laws institutionalized discrimination against Roman Catholics in Ireland, the Croagh Patrick pilgrimage was a focus of defiance and attempts to suppress it met with fierce resistance. Today the hard climb up the rocky slopes of Croagh Patrick continues to be a popular pilgrimage, particularly on the last Sunday in July when more than 25,000 visit the mountain. As a sign of devotion and penance, some pilgrims walk barefoot to the summit.

I have strong memories of our afternoon on Croagh Patrick. As we ascended the well-worn path, a cloud gradually shrouded the summit above, and soon we, too, were enveloped in mist. What had seemed like a straightforward climb just a few minutes before now became more dangerous as we began to worry about losing our way. Croagh Patrick, we decided, is still a place of power, and we were not entirely sorry to turn around and head back toward shelter.

Another Irish site with great resonance for pilgrims is Glendalough, located twenty miles south of Dublin. Nestled like an Irish Brigadoon in the Wicklow

Mountains, Glendalough preserves the remains of a settlement established by St. Kevin in the sixth century. Its buildings include a round tower, church, priest's house, several High Crosses, and a beehive-shaped hut, all dating from the eighth to twelfth centuries.

Perhaps no other Celtic site gives as much of a sense for what the early monastic communities were like as Glendalough. Throughout this period, monasteries filled the role that parish churches would later claim, serving as the primary focus for worship, community, and religious instruction. These settlements often contained both men and women, lay and ordained. While they provided places of retreat from the bustle of the world, they were also intimately involved in the lives of local people in the community, filling the roles of hospital, school, guest house, and center for the arts as well as a place for worship and prayer.

Like Iona, Glendalough attracts growing numbers of pilgrims. Several retreat centers offer guided programs and rooms for solitary pilgrimages. A network of trails winds throughout the serene mountain valley, providing many places for prayer and contemplation.

The spirit of St. Kevin is as present here as St. Columba is on Iona. Kevin has been called a Celtic St. Francis, a holy man known for his love of the birds and beasts. A favorite legend says that a bird once built a nest in his hand as his arms were outstretched in prayer. Loathe to disturb her, Kevin kept his arms in place until the little birds had hatched. Among the sites associated with Kevin in the Glendalough valley are a small cave known as St. Kevin's Bed, a place where he retreated for prayer, and St. Kevin's Cell, a small building that is said to have been his home.

In England, the primary pilgrimage site for those seeking to follow in the footsteps of Celtic Christians is Lindisfarne, also known as Holy Island. Located off the coast of Northumberland in the north of England, Lindisfarne was founded in 635 by the Irish monk Aidan, who had received his religious training on Iona. The monastery rapidly became a renowned center for learning. In 698 the body of St. Cuthbert was enshrined here, making this an even more important spot for pilgrims.

Cuthbert was a beloved figure in the early Celtic church. He served as prior at Lindisfarne for a number of years before withdrawing to the nearby tiny island of Inner Farne, a place where he could escape from all worldly distractions and temptations. Though he loved his solitary life, he was persuaded to return to Lindisfarne as bishop in 685. There he pursued an active life of pastoral care and constant journeying around his large diocese.

A number of wonderful legends are associated with Cuthbert, many reflecting the Celtic love for birds, beasts, and the rest of the natural world. One of my favorites explains why the saint is frequently depicted with otters. The story is told in a biography of the saint written by Bede, an eighth-century church historian. Cuthbert would often disappear from the monastery to spend the night in prayer by the seashore. One night another monk followed him and watched as Cuthbert waded into the water and stayed there for hours, praising God. At dawn Cuthbert returned to the shore, fell to his knees, and began to pray again. While he was doing this, two otters came out of the sea and breathed upon his feet, rubbing them with their fur to warm them. After Cuthbert blessed them, they returned to the sea, and ever since the saint has been associated with the animal.

When Cuthbert died, he was buried near the altar in St. Peter's Church on Lindisfarne. Eleven years later, monks disinterred his body to transfer it to a new shrine and discovered to their surprise that his remains had not decayed or crumbled. Taking this as a sign of Cuthbert's saintliness, the monks reburied his body in the floor of the church, and Lindisfarne became a focus of pilgrimage for those seeking his relics. The Lindisfarne Gospels, an illuminated manuscript created about 698, gave the settlement additional fame.

Over the next century Lindisfarne grew in wealth and influence as pilgrims poured onto the island. Kings and noblemen donated land as well as money and precious objects. It was inevitable that the isolated, wealthy settlement would become the target of the Vikings, who sacked the island in 793. Some said that it was a judgment by God against the luxurious lifestyle of the monks and the ways in which they had fallen away from the holy path. News of the disaster spread as far away as the court of Charlemagne, the greatest ruler in Europe. Within a generation the monks of Lindisfarne had left Holy Island, eventually taking the remains of Cuthbert to the Cathedral at Durham.

Cuthbert continued to be a much-revered figure in the north of England. Both Lindisfarne and the island of Farne were often visited by pilgrims, and some monks chose to follow in his footsteps by becoming hermits at these sites. During the twelfth century, the church on Holy Island was reconstructed and other monastic buildings were begun. The church had a presence here throughout the Middle Ages, until Henry VIII dissolved the monastery system in 1536. Lindisfarne continued to be a place of prayer and retreat, however, and its village church has served as a focus for worship for many generations. Today several denominations run retreat programs on the island.

Because Lindisfarne is an island at high tide, pilgrims need to time their visit to when the road leading to it is

free of water. Travelers can wander amid the ruins, tour Lindisfarne Castle, visit local churches and a museum, and walk along the shore as St. Cuthbert did so long ago. Appropriately enough, part of the island is now a nature preserve—something that would undoubtedly have pleased Cuthbert.

Lindisfarne, Glendalough, Iona, and the St. Patrick-related sites of Ireland represent only a sampling of pilgrimage sites relating to Celtic Christianity. Among other important sites are Skellig Michael, a pinnacle of rock off the coast of County Kerry that once housed an isolated monastery; Glencolumbkille in County Donegal, a popular place of pilgrimage because of its association with St. Columba; and Monasterboice in County Louth, site of monastic ruins and exquisitely carved, tenth-century High Crosses.

Travelers will find many of these High Crosses throughout Ireland. Formed with a ring encircling their arms, they feature elaborately carved Biblical scenes. The crosses were teaching tools for Christians, but they also served as boundary markers, preaching stations, and symbols of prestige for monasteries. Standing as high as twenty feet, the crosses continue to be beacons for prayer and landmarks for travelers.

Finally, no pilgrimage to Ireland would be complete without visiting the library at Trinity College in Dublin where the *Book of Kells* is kept. Exhibits there detail the laborious steps that went into the creation of the illuminated manuscript that is the foremost treasure of Celtic

Christianity. On its vellum pages, the four Gospels are brought to vivid, colorful life with fantastically elaborate decorations.

Viewing the *Book of Kells* is one of my favorite memories of Ireland, for as I stood before its pages I felt as if I was indeed in a place where the veil between worlds was thin.

In *The Celtic Way* Ian Bradley chooses the image of the Celtic knot to illustrate the character of the early Christian church in Britain. This design of endlessly looping and interlacing ribbons is found throughout Celtic art, adorning High Crosses and filling the pages of illuminated manuscripts. The motif is of pre-Christian origin and likely symbolized the endless cycle of existence. In the Christian era it became a symbol of eternity and also of protection, for the Celts believed that the Devil was frustrated by anything that went on forever and didn't have a definitive beginning and end. (This was one reason why the Celts considered the constantly moving waters of springs and rivers as holy spots.)

The Celtic knot has another feature, a clearly defined border that encloses the spiral within. Bradley writes that the combination of constant movement within the knot, and the sense of boundary and protection given by the border, makes it an apt metaphor for the appeal of Celtic spirituality.

Writes Bradley: "We too can both lose and find ourselves as pilgrims within the twists and turns of the Celtic knot . . . If it seems a mass of detours and diversions, false trails and cul de sacs, then that is the way that the Lord marked out for his pilgrim people Israel when he led them out of Egypt not on the most direct track but by a roundabout route. If it offers endless opportunities along the way, it is also the path of waiting and suffering, disappointments and frustrations, the *via dolorosa* which leads to the Cross. In the end it brings us back to where we began, to the one who is the Alpha and Omega, the beginning and the end of our journey."

And so from these early Celtic Christians we are reminded that our entire lives are to be spent on pilgrimage. We may at times seem to wander aimlessly, looping and circling back upon ourselves, lost in frustration and disappointments, but all of our journeys are contained within the protective embrace of God.

In the words of a traditional Celtic blessing:

Be each saint in heaven,
Each sainted woman in heaven,
Each angel in heaven
Stretching their arms for you,
Smoothing the way for you,
When you go thither
   Over the river hard to see;
Oh when you go thither home
   Over the river hard to see.

4

Sacred Lands
Normandy and Bear Butte

A LL cemeteries are sacred places, but there is a special poignancy about a certain windswept military cemetery that lies above the English Channel in northern France. Buried there are 9,387 soldiers killed during the invasion of Normandy during World War II. Row upon row of sons, husbands, and fathers rest in this peaceful spot where the only sounds are the raucous call of sea gulls and the muted crash of waves.

The serene atmosphere is a contrast to the violence that reigned here on June 6, 1944. On that date—better known as D-Day—Allied forces launched the largest amphibious landing in history on the coast of Normandy, a massive assault that included 156,000 soldiers, 7,000 ships, and nearly 12,000 aircraft. On the beach below where the orderly marble headstones now stand, thousands of men lost their lives. While that stretch of sand has a French name, it is far better known by the designation given it by Allied military commanders: Omaha Beach.

A trip to Normandy shows that more than just religious sites inspire pilgrimages. Omaha Beach and the

American Cemetery above it are hallowed not because of their connection to a saint, but because of the ordinary men who fought and gave their lives here.

Other battlefields have a similar air of hushed reverence—Gettysburg in Pennsylvania, for example, and the Little Bighorn Battlefield in Montana—but the D-Day sites of Normandy possess a particular power because they are part of the living memory of so many Americans. Even if we have no direct connection to the men who fought on these beaches, many of us have traveled to this spot in our imaginations through television and film. We know about the bravery of those young men who walked into gunfire as they came across the sand, watching their comrades fall all around them as the water turned red with blood. Heroism is a concept we often trivialize in our culture, but in Normandy we honor genuine bravery.

Each year thousands of people tour the D-Day sites of northern France. They retrace the route taken by the soldiers on the beaches, not only on Omaha but also on Utah, Gold, Juno and Sword Beaches. They stand high above the ocean at Pointe du Hoc, seeing the ground that still bears the deep crevices created by bombs as they marvel at the bravery of the U.S. Army Rangers who climbed the point's sheer cliff amid enemy fire. They walk among the graves at the American cemetery, reading the names of the young soldiers, listening to the sea gulls, smelling the salt air, and imagining what it was like here on that June day in 1944.

The number of veterans coming here is dwindling, say local residents. By now many in that "greatest generation" have died, while most of those who remain are too old and infirm to make the journey. But other visitors are taking their place, as the World War II sites continue to exercise fascination. Some come because of movies like *Saving Private Ryan* and *Band of Brothers*, action films that make them want to see the landscape behind the stories. Others tour the D-Day sites simply as a way to spend an afternoon while on holiday.

Those who come here on pilgrimage have deeper reasons. Many have a father or grandfather who fought in Normandy, and their visit gives them an insight into their loved one's experiences in the war. Even those without a direct personal connection can make a meaningful pilgrimage to Normandy, a trip that honors the courage of a generation now nearly gone and makes us ponder a war that shaped much of our modern world.

My own experiences in Normandy were greatly enhanced by a local tour guide, Francois Gauthron, who took a friend and me to the major sites connected with D-Day. A veteran of the French military and native of the area, Francois has been leading tours in Normandy for the past decade. He has taken thousands of American veterans back to the sites where they fought in the war, helping them retrace their steps across the beaches, down country roads, and across fields where cattle now graze. A number of times he has been able to reunite veterans with locals who remembered them from the war years. Showing up unannounced in a village, they will be warmly welcomed by people who still remember the young American soldiers who liberated them during the Normandy campaign.

One gets the sense from such anecdotes that a pilgrimage like this can complete a story begun long ago. For many of these men, the last time they saw France was when it was under attack, ravaged by bombs and gunfire. For them the prosperous farms and tidy villages of Normandy today likely seem like a vindication for the sacrifices and hardships they endured as young men, proof that peace can flourish after the horrors of war.

The most touching story told by Francois took place about ten years ago, a time when many veterans were returning to Normandy for the fiftieth anniversary of D-Day. Because most were in their 70s, the men knew it would likely be their last chance to make the journey.

Francois' story took place during a reunion of an American bomber squadron, which hired him to take them to sites connected with their war experiences. One evening Francois ended a long day of touring by taking the men to a local bar. The room already contained quite a few people when they entered, most of them men about the same age as the veterans. When Francois heard that they were speaking German, he guessed that they were veterans from the other side of the conflict.

Conferring with the group's guide, he received confirmation of his surmise. "Your guys dropped bombs on my guys during the war," the other guide told him. "This could get interesting."

As the American vets entered the room, Francois watched with a bit of apprehension. It didn't take the Americans long to overhear the conversations in German and figure out who the men were. There was a period of awkwardness as the veterans found seats, and then finally one of the Americans went over to a table where some of the elderly Germans were sitting. He introduced himself in German and struck up a conversation. Soon another veteran did the same.

"After about ten minutes, everybody in the room was talking to each other and sharing stories," Francois recalled. "The Germans talked about what it was like to be young and scared that the next bomb was going to land on them, and the Americans told them what it was like to be young and scared as they flew planes amid anti-aircraft fire. For two hours they talked non-stop, and at the end of the evening they exchanged addresses with each other. I wouldn't be surprised if some of them are still corresponding to this day."

For those men, Americans and Germans alike, their war finally ended over glasses of beer in a French bar, more than fifty years after the armistice had been signed.

The story illustrates the ways in which a pilgrimage can help us lay to rest ghosts that linger from many years past. For some travelers those ghosts might linger from war experiences in Korea or Vietnam, for others from the lingering pain after a divorce or family estrangement. On our journeys the healing process can be triggered by seemingly chance encounters that allow us to finally release the burdens of memory we carry.

While battlefields are hallowed by blood and sacrifice, other secular locations can also take on the deeper meaning of a pilgrimage site. The monuments that line the Mall in Washington, D.C., have such an aura, as does Ellis Island in New York where many immigrants entered the United States. Pop culture has its pilgrimage sites as well, of course, from Elvis Presley's Graceland in Memphis to Abbey Road in London, where the Beatles made their early recordings.

For me Springfield, Illinois, is a place of pilgrimage because of its association with one of my heroes, Abraham Lincoln. As a child I remember becoming fascinated by the story of Lincoln, memorizing the Gettysburg Address and reading stories of his life. That interest has continued to blossom as an adult, and when I finally had the chance to visit the small city where Lincoln lived for much of his adult life, the experience was more than an ordinary trip for me.

There's an impressive new museum in Springfield that tells Lincoln's story through multi-media exhibits, but to me the most moving parts of our tour came while visiting the historic sites associated with his life, particularly the home where he lived for seventeen years and the Old State Capitol where he served as a legislator and a lawyer. Something about walking the same well-worn wooden floors that Lincoln had trod brought his spirit alive for me in a way I'd never felt before.

That experience helped me better understand the significance of relics in the history of pilgrimage. Especially during the Middle Ages, many pilgrims sought out churches that claimed to have a saint's relic such as a bone or a piece of cloth. Other religious traditions have this practice as well, particularly Buddhism (many temples contain stupas that hold a relic of the Buddha or of another venerated figure). There seems to be a deep human longing to have a physical connection to a person of holiness, a belief that some of their spirit can be transmitted through an object belonging to them.

Such devotion can become corrupt, of course. The medieval trade in relics became scandalous as churches vied for items (authentic or not) that would bring them wealth and power. But the original impulse to venerate a relic is an understandable one. For me, standing at the various Lincoln sites—particularly his tomb—gave me a sense of connection beyond what I'd found in history books. Many of us seek such a connection on our travels, wanting something that will continue to inspire us once we leave that holy ground.

And so places like Normandy, the Lincoln sites in Springfield, and national monuments like the Vietnam Veterans Memorial can all function as pilgrimage sites. While not explicitly religious, they allow us to connect our stories to a larger national narrative, challenging us to greater idealism and commitment.

For many of us, natural places can also be holy and hallowed. Many generations of pilgrims have found solace and inspiration at places like the Grand Canyon, the Great Sand Dunes in Colorado, and the redwood forests of California. Something about the innate character of such places can bring us out of ourselves and our mundane concerns, opening our hearts to something deeper and richer.

For me, Bear Butte in western South Dakota is such a place. The site is technically not a butte, but rather a small mountain that stands just east of the Black Hills. It is both a state park and a holy site for many Plains Indians tribes, including the Lakota and the Cheyenne.

Surrounded by prairie, it is formed from volcanic rock that has been worn into its present shape over millions of years. The Lakota people call it *Mato Paha* or "bear mountain," a reference to the fact that its profile on the horizon resembles a sleeping bear.

Bear Butte is steeped in Indian lore and history. Revered leaders like Red Cloud, Crazy Horse, and Sitting Bull all visited the site to pray, and it continues to be a place of pilgrimage for Native Americans throughout the United States and Canada. Vision quests, sweat lodges, and other ceremonies are frequently held on the mountain.

Even for a casual hiker, evidence of the mountain's unique character is everywhere. Along the two-mile path to its summit are many trees and bushes tied with pieces of cloth and strings containing tiny bundles of tobacco, which is regarded as a sacred herb by Indians. Some of the offerings are faded and weathered by the sun, while others are clearly recent. At the base of the mountain is an area reserved for Indian ceremonial use, and often you can hear the sound of drums as you climb the mountain, a compelling counterpoint to the ceaseless whisper of the prairie wind.

Because my husband's family lives near Bear Butte, I have visited this place many times. Over the years I have come to love this worn and ancient mountain, and my experiences, I think, highlight some important aspects of pilgrimage.

One is that a pilgrimage to a particular place is often a ritual that we repeat again and again. I have hiked the trail to the summit of Bear Butte nearly every summer for the past 20 years. When I first came to the mountain, I was a young woman. Later I hiked it while pregnant, then while carrying my small son in a pack on my back. Today in middle age I hike it more slowly, but with an even deeper appreciation for its power and beauty.

For me, then, Bear Butte is a holy place in part because I have made it so. Since I come here only once a year, my annual visit is a natural time to reflect on the passage of time. I journey here while on vacation, when my mind is not so cluttered by day-to-day details and commitments. I come with an open heart, eager to experience its beauty once again and reflect on the year that has passed.

I suspect that the power of this place is not apparent to many of the people who visit here. As mountains go, it's pretty small and unimpressive. Because it is so exposed to the elements, the hot sun and nearly constant wind can be merciless in the summer. There are far more scenic places in the Black Hills, sites where tourists flock for much of the year.

Yet this is clearly a holy place. Part of its holiness derives from the fact that so many people have come here for religious inspiration for so many centuries. Like a medieval cathedral hallowed by generations of worshipers, the mountain is steeped in countless prayers. The prayer flags flapping in the wind are constant reminders that many pilgrims have passed this way before.

The sacredness of this spot is also due, I think, to the fact that the mountain is immensely old. Its spine of igneous rock was formed sixty million years ago, gradually emerging from the earth as the softer layers of shale around it were eroded. In a world that constantly celebrates the new and novel, ancient places like Bear Butte are reminders of how fleeting our lives are. While in our personal lives we shift homes and even identities at will, constantly re-creating who we are, we still yearn for the deep roots that only the passing of many years can provide. When we find a place that is of great age, it speaks to us at some deep and unconscious level.

Finally, part of Bear Butte's power comes from the fact that it is a mountain, which humans have always viewed with awe and wonder. Standing in isolation, it forms a natural landmark on the dry prairies of South Dakota, visible from many miles away. Landmarks like these have often become places of special power. The Bible contains many references to mountains that are associated with the holy, including Mount Sinai, Mount Carmel, and Mount Tabor. These high places are natural places for pilgrimage, calling us to remove ourselves from our ordinary lives and ascend to a different realm.

"It seems to me that a mountain is an image of the soul as it lifts itself up in contemplation," wrote St. Theodore of Studium in the ninth century, speaking to monks who had fled from persecution to the safety of the mountains. "For in the same manner as the mountain towers above the valleys and lowlands at its foot, so does the soul of [the one] who prays mount into the higher regions up to God. You are the Lord's eagles, who wing your flights high in the ethereal regions."

The words of Psalm 121 put it more simply: "I lift up my eyes to the hills—from where will my help come? My help comes from the Lord, who made heaven and earth."

Ten years ago, my husband and I were greatly distressed to hear the news that a wildfire had swept across Bear Butte, incinerating more than ninety percent of its trees and vegetation. The images of the devastation we saw in the newspaper made us heartsick, for we knew how much beauty had been destroyed in the space of just a few hours. When we had the chance to return the following summer, it was with great trepidation. We worried that a place we loved had been spoiled, for the mountain would never look the same again (at least in our lifetimes).

That first visit back was indeed a shock. Blackened trees stood forlornly along the trail, some already toppled by the wind. But amid the devastation, new life was blossoming. Fire is an engine of regeneration in nature, releasing nutrients back into the soil and stimulating new growth in many plants and seeds. Scattered among the blackened trunks were beautiful wildflowers and a dazzling array of butterflies. The mountain was different than what we had experienced before, but it was still a holy place for us.

Since the fire of 1996 we have returned each year to Bear Butte, viewing its regeneration with fascination. Each time we see more evidence of new life emerging from the rocky ground of the mountain. It didn't surprise us to learn that some Native Americans viewed the fire on Bear Butte as a necessary cleansing of the mountain. It does indeed feel purified, stripped down to its backbone of rock and soil.

On our annual visit to Bear Butte, I often recall how it looked when I first saw it two decades ago. I remember the tall pine trees that covered much of its surface, and how cool their shade felt in the heat of a summer afternoon. Now more than ever before, this place speaks to me of both permanence and impermanence. What is holy remains, and what is superfluous returns to dust. Surely that is one of the most important lessons that one can learn from pilgrimage.

I have made my teenage sons promise me that when they are old men, they will return to Bear Butte at least once to see the mountain as it was when I first viewed it. They have agreed to this solemn command with the casualness of youth, clearly humoring their slightly daft mother. But sixty years from now, I want them to see the pine trees growing tall once again on Bear Butte, providing cool shade in the heat of a Dakota summer. The prairie winds will dance around the summit, stirring the prayer flags tied by pilgrims. I hope my sons will cast their own prayers into that wind as they remember how much their parents loved this worn and ancient mountain.

5

The Pilgrim's Way
Japan and South Korea

W HEN I think back to my trips exploring Buddhist sites in South Korea and Japan, what comes to my mind first is the sound of bells: softly tinkling, muted chimes, blowing gently in the wind in mountaintop monasteries. Something about the peacefulness of that melodious sound captures for me the spirit of those retreats. When I hear the sound of bells now I am transported back, and for a time I can recall the deep serenity I encountered in the holy sites of those countries.

My trips to Asia have given me an invaluable window into Buddhism, a religion from which I have learned a great deal. My experiences there relate, I think, to a common phenomenon among pilgrims: though we are rooted in one faith, we can often sense a kinship with the spiritual traditions of another. That kinship is especially evident on a visit to sacred sites. Many of us have stood in a holy place foreign to us, and yet something about the atmosphere seemed familiar. Though the rituals and iconography may be very different from what we are accustomed to, we can sense the sacredness of the space, something that speaks directly to our hearts in a way that goes deeper than language.

Equally intriguing are the bonds that can spring up between strangers while we are traveling. Help and guidance often come from unexpected sources while we are on the pilgrim's path. In the space of a brief encounter, the sacred can enter our lives, creating a luminous moment of connection and insight. We stop to ask directions from a woman on the side of the road and end up having a conversation that helps us discern the next step on our interior journey as well as our outward one. The stranger who takes a seat next to us becomes a valued friend for the rest of the journey or perhaps for the rest of our lives. Our task is to be attentive, to listen, and to welcome the holy when it finds us.

My interest in Buddhism began long before I visited Japan, but my visit there greatly deepened my respect for that venerable tradition. While I was impressed by many aspects of Japan—in particular its artistic treasures, enormous energy, and great natural beauty—I found myself most drawn to its spiritual traditions.

I remember my first glimpse of Mount Fuji, the sacred mountain of Japan. I had seen its image before, of course, for the snow-topped peak is probably the most photographed place in all of Asia. But seeing its beauty in person made the breath catch in my throat. Along with countless other travelers throughout the centuries, I could sense that there was something otherworldly about this mountain, which has been a holy place for the Japanese from time immemorial.

In Shintoism—the indigenous, shamanistic religion of Japan—mountains are believed to be the dwelling places of gods and spirits, mysterious places that must be approached with awe and great care. It's not surprising, then, that Mount Fuji would be held in special reverence, both because it is the tallest mountain in Japan and because of its great beauty. Formed from an ancient volcano, Mount Fuji is nearly perfectly symmetrical and rises far higher than the surrounding mountains. On a clear day it can be viewed from a distance of a hundred miles, dominating the landscape of much of central Japan. Its iconic image has been portrayed in countless paintings and has been celebrated by poets through many generations, making it the universally recognized symbol of Japan.

Mount Fuji has been a place of pilgrimage for centuries (though it was only in 1867 that women were first allowed to climb it). Tradition said that the goddess of the mountain would throw from her side any climber who was not pure of heart. Today, as in centuries past, climbers time their ascent so that they can watch the sunrise from the top. The climb, which is typically done in July and August, is not easy. In fact, the Japanese say that everyone should climb Mount Fuji once, but to climb it twice is foolish.

While I toured Japan at the wrong time of year to hike to the top of the mountain, I was fortunate to have the chance to visit Mount Fuji on a clear day when its summit was unobscured by clouds. We were able to ascend part of the way to one of the stations that serve pilgrims and tourists. Even such a brief visit gave me a sense for the ethereal, remote spirit of Mount Fuji. While much of Japan had initially seemed Westernized and relentlessly busy, on this sacred mountain I could glimpse the calm stillness that lies at the heart of Japanese culture.

I felt that stillness even more powerfully in the Buddhist temples I visited during my stay. The most striking were located in the mountains high above the development that fills most valleys in Japan. Many temples are actually a complex of buildings, often including a main hall for worship, a pagoda containing a sacred relic, a lecture hall, a huge bell hanging in its own separate structure, and massive gates marking the entrance. These Japanese temples have a spare, simple beauty very different from the splendor of Christian cathedrals, but they evoke a similar response of reverence.

Visiting the holy sites of another tradition often causes us to question our own assumptions. I remember being taken aback by a scene at Minobusan Temple in the mountains of Yamanashi Prefecture, where I encountered a robed monk standing silently by the entrance holding a begging bowl in his hand. In America, those who beg for food are poor and destitute, the most marginalized in our society. Instead the man before me was young and strong, obviously in the peak of health. Our guide explained that the monks at the temple begged for donations as a way of encouraging humility and also to give visitors the chance to experience the blessing of giving. As the monk stood ramrod-straight and expressionless in front of us, his eyes downcast, he was a silent witness to a tradition very different from my own. I realized how little my own culture values humility, and how in countless ways we are encouraged instead to guard and protect our egos.

Of all my experiences in Japan, the most intriguing was my introduction to the tea ceremony, that quintessential Japanese art form. The tea ceremony is simply that: the preparation of tea that is served to guests. But within that most ordinary of activities, a wealth of ritual and an entire religious philosophy are contained.

Tea came to Japan from China in the tenth century, and the popular new drink soon became another way for the upper classes to display their wealth by using expensive utensils arranged in elaborate settings. Beginning in the fourteenth century, however, Buddhist masters developed the tea ceremony as a spiritual practice, a ritual that embodied the Zen esthetic and philosophy. Using plain implements and delicate, graceful movements, a student practiced the ritual to awaken to the beauty to be found in the everyday. While the tea ceremony demands total attention to detail, in that focus there is a kind of paradoxical freedom of the spirit.

What looks simple from the outside is actually very difficult to practice, I discovered when I participated in a tea ceremony class. As my teacher patiently explained the precise order of the ritual, I proceeded to make a fool of myself, clanging the utensils together, spilling some of the tea, and immediately forgetting the steps that I had been told to follow. My legs hurt from kneeling and my borrowed kimono kept coming undone. If ever there was an activity designed to make one feel like a graceless clod, surely the tea ceremony is it, I concluded. And yet at the end when I was finally able to sit back and observe the teacher do the ritual properly, I found myself transported by the elegant beauty of her movements. I could see why someone would study this spiritual practice for years, for in the actions there was a meditative ease that I had never encountered before.

One of the first Western descriptions of the tea ceremony, written by Portuguese Jesuit Juan Rodriguez, is still a good summation of its essential nature: the ritual is designed to "produce courtesy, politeness, modesty, exterior moderation, calmness, peace of body and soul without any pride or arrogance, fleeing from all ostentation, pomp, external grandeur and magnificence."

We in the West who are relentlessly busy and perpetually stressed, who feed ourselves with food and drink so rapidly that we barely notice what we are wolfing down, would do well to heed the lessons of the tea ceremony.

While Japan intrigued me, South Korea captured my heart. Part of it was the warmth of the Korean people, who made me feel welcome wherever I traveled. I was also moved by the beauty and soulfulness of Korea, that land that has so often been torn by war and that is still divided by a fiercely guarded border. Strategically located between Japan and China and often invaded by powerful empires, Korea has managed to forge its own unique, complex culture.

Two places in particular captured my imagination and spoke eloquently to the pilgrim in me. The first was the ancient royal city of Gyeongju, which was for a thousand years the capital of the Silla Kingdom in central Korea. Along with Kyoto in Japan, Gyeongju has been designated by UNESCO as one of the world's ten most important ancient cultural cities. From the first to the tenth centuries, Gyeongju reigned as the spiritual, cultural, and political heart of the Korean peninsula, a city of immense wealth and power.

Pilgrims who visit Gyeongju today will find that it is an immense museum without walls, a place where the past is constantly visible. Burial mounds, temple sites, rock sculptures, and the ruins of fortresses and pagodas fill the city and surrounding area. Gyeongju's beauty is enhanced by the fact that it is far less congested than many cities in Korea, with tree-lined streets and colorful flowers. No where else does the spirit of ancient Korea seem as vibrant and immediate, making it one of the most visited destinations in the country.

The most visible signs of Gyeongju's illustrious past are burial tombs. Nearly 700 have been discovered within the city and its outskirts. Some have been excavated, revealing rich caches of jewelry, weapons, decorative items, earthenware, and other artifacts. The best place to view them is Tumulus Park on the southern edge of the downtown. The park offers a serene place to stroll amid more than a dozen of the grass-covered mounds, some rising to heights of seventy-five feet. One of the mounds has been turned into a small museum, allowing visitors to walk inside its inner chamber and see reproductions of the exquisitely crafted jewelry and weaponry that were found inside.

Travelers can see the originals of these and other artifacts at the Gyeongju National Museum, which gives additional background on the sophisticated civilization that existed here for a millennium. Outside the entrance to the museum hangs the largest and most beloved bell in Korea: the Emille Bell, cast in 771 by a king of the Silla Kingdom. The huge, embellished bell hangs over a shallow echo chamber, which amplifies its sound when struck. The bell's name comes from a tragic legend associated with its creation. When the bell was first made, it failed to ring. After the metal was melted down and the bell remade, it cracked when it was struck for the first time. The head priest of a local temple had a dream in which a spirit appeared to him, saying that the fire spirit dragon needed to be appeased in order for the bell to sound. The bell should be melted down once again, only this time a young girl was to be sacrificed into the molten metal before the bell was recast. The terrible deed was done, and ever since when struck the bell is said to echo the cries of the girl, who as she died screamed "emille," or "mother" in the language of the Silla.

Stories like this illustrate the ways in which echoes of the past live on in Gyeongju today. Like many pilgrimage sites, this is a place where the dead are not forgotten. Walking amid the ancient tombs and structures, a traveler can feel a peculiar interweaving of time, as if the twenty-first century is merely the thinnest overlay on a far older tradition that still beats just beneath the surface.

The most famous landmark of the Gyeongju region is found in the mountains that lie to the east of the city. Seokguram, a grotto containing a white granite image of the Buddha, sits atop a forested mountain and has been a place of pilgrimage for the Korean people for many centuries. The image is the crowning glory of the Silla Kingdom, a work of stunning artistic beauty and deep religious significance that is considered one of Korea's national treasures.

Built in 751, the grotto is carved into the side of the mountain and for hundreds of years was open to the elements (glass now protects the inner chamber). The Buddha that is its focus rests on a pedestal decorated with carved lotus flowers, with an array of religious figures depicted on the encircling walls. The figure is believed to be one of the guardians of Korea, protecting the land from invasion from across the sea.

Standing before the figure, its beauty seemed almost luminescent, in part because of the whiteness of the stone. I had never been in the presence of anything that exuded such a sense of peace. Though the religious art of Christianity is powerful and varied and beautiful, I couldn't recall anything that could equal the serenity of the Buddha before me.

While this sacred site high in the mountains of South Korea felt foreign in many ways, two things seemed familiar: the hushed and reverent atmosphere within the grotto and the rapt expressions of the people gathered in prayer. Though the words they were chanting were unknown to me, their attitude of devotion was not. A common bond unites pilgrims of all faiths, despite differences of culture and belief. Perhaps in that fact, there is hope that we may yet learn to bridge the religious differences that divide the peoples of the world.

Of all my experiences traveling in Asia, the most powerful came during an overnight stay at Beomeosa Temple in the southern part of South Korea. A seemingly chance encounter became a powerful illustration of what can happen on pilgrimage if one is open to the grace of unexpected connections.

Founded in 678, Beomeosa Temple perches near the top of a mountain near the port city of Busan. About 150 monks live in the main temple complex and in smaller temples and hermitages scattered throughout the surrounding forest. Beomeosa is one of the largest temples in South Korea, with most of its present buildings dating from the seventeenth and eighteenth centuries. Its monks practice a form of Buddhism called Seon in Korean (better known as Zen in the west).

Along with nearly fifty other Buddhist temples in South Korea, Beomeosa offers a temple stay program that allows visitors to experience the lifestyle of a monk. The experience is one I would recommend to any traveler, though it was not without difficulties. Even on a twenty-four-hour visit, it is possible to get a sense for the rigorous demands of this spiritual path. By its end I felt a sense of genuine awe for the monks who live at Beomeosa. If one uses the metaphor of athletic competition in relation to religious life, these men are at the level of Olympic athletes, honed mentally, physically, and spiritually by a lifestyle that demands total dedication and commitment.

After arriving at Beomeosa late in the afternoon, my group of about thirty Americans was led by our guide through the temple complex. I looked with interest at its several dozen wooden buildings, most with ornately painted exteriors and tile roofs. The smell of incense and the sound of tinkling bells filled the air, and inside several buildings I glimpsed golden statues and flickering candles. Several robed monks with shaven heads walked through the compound, their eyes downcast and their hands folded together inside their sleeves.

Our first task was to put on our own monastic attire, a loose-fitting gray vest and trousers that went over our clothes. While before we had looked like tourists, the change in costume gave us a sense of kinship with the monks in their gray robes. I was reminded of the fact that in many traditions pilgrims wear special clothing or other items to set them apart. Before setting off for Jerusalem, medieval Christians would sew crosses onto their cloaks to identify themselves as pilgrims. Travelers to Santiago de Compostela wear the shell as a symbol of their journey; Muslims traveling to Mecca wear white.

Once we were all clad in gray, we were given an orientation to the monastery's schedule. At one point the guide paused to ask for a volunteer to read an informative passage projected onto the wall. I was among several people who raised their hand, and the woman called on me. After I finished reading, she crossed the room to give me a large, flat cardboard box.

"This is a gift from the abbot of the monastery to you," she said.

Taken aback, I accepted the wrapped package with thanks and set it aside to open later. It remained there as we moved on to the next part of the program, in which a monk instructed us in monastic etiquette—how to stand, walk, bow, and perform the full-body prostration that is part of the monks' prayer rituals. The man had the air of a wise sage, and as he waited for his words to be translated by the interpreter he looked steadily at us, his gaze piercing.

When the instructions were completed, our group prepared to leave for the dining hall. One of the temple assistants, a middle-aged woman with a kind face, came up to me.

"You must be a special person to be chosen to receive this gift from the abbot," she said, pointing to the box in my hands. "Inside is a handmade calendar with photographs taken by one of the monks here. He is both a monk and a famous photographer in Korea."

While I was flattered by her words, I felt obliged to point out that I had obviously been picked by chance to receive the gift. The guide had likely chosen me because I was closest to the screen, I said.

The woman shook her head, smiling. "I do not think you were given this gift by chance," she said. Then she asked if I was interested in meeting the monk who had taken the photographs. When I nodded enthusiastically, she said that she would try to arrange it before we left the next day.

"Now you must hurry to get to the dining hall," she said.

As I walked down the hill, I reflected on the woman's words. Surely the calendar had been given at random, I thought. The abbot had likely wanted to give a gift to the entire group as a gesture of hospitality, and the guide had been told to pick someone. As much as I wanted to believe some mystical force was at work, I doubted it was so.

The dining rituals soon drove all other thoughts out of my mind. In a spare and unfurnished room, we settled onto mats arranged in two long lines. Hye Su, the monk who had instructed us earlier, now explained the temple's eating ceremony. In deference to all of those who are hungry in the world, we were told to take only seventy percent of what would make us full.

"Eat everything you take," he added. "If any food is left at the end, it will be put into the waste water and we will all consume it."

He can't be serious, I thought—and then changed my mind as I looked at his stern expression.

While not gourmet quality, the food was nutritious and filling: tofu, vegetables, rice, and soup. At the end we scrubbed our bowls with a slice of Japanese radish and— with a sigh and a gulp—drank the rinse water we had used to clean our bowls. I was relieved to see that everyone had finished the last morsels of their meal.

Back at the guest house, Hye Su continued our instruction in Buddhism. "If you are happy, you do not need to practice Buddhism," he said. "But if you are unhappy, it can show you the way to escape the bonds of desire. Happiness comes from knowing your true self."

I found myself increasingly fascinated by this man with the piercing gaze. During the question and answer period that followed his instruction, several in my group asked questions about his background. He had entered the monastery at sixteen, he said, following the example of his older brother.

"How often do you get the chance to see your family?" someone in our group asked.

A smile broke across his normally reserved face. "You are all my family," he said, gesturing to us. "You are my brothers and sisters."

My stay at the monastery was a mixture of fascination and exhaustion. Everything seemed exotic and intriguing, but the physical rigors of the experience surprised me. Kneeling on a hard floor is difficult for bodies used to sitting on chairs, while the full-body prostrations were fun for the first five times, tedious for the next twenty, and excruciating by the time I had done thirty.

The early morning wake-up call was a challenge as well. Bright lights were turned on in the guest house at 3:00 a.m., as a half-dozen female temple volunteers hurried in to help us fold up our futons. Stumbling into the darkness, a few minutes later we made our way down the hillside to a raised platform that contained a hanging drum at least ten feet in diameter. As a monk approached it and began to pound its surface, the sound reverberated through the night air. The wild, throbbing drumming went on for nearly a half hour, gradually bringing our sleepy minds to greater clarity.

Next it was time for morning prayers in a meditation hall lined with tatami mats. About twenty monks were already in place when we entered, standing silently on their cushions. Once our group was in place, they began to chant in Korean, their deep voices blending in a seamless melody. Every few minutes they dropped to the floor to do a full-body prostration, a movement that we Westerners awkwardly emulated.

Out of the corner of my eye I watched the monks, intrigued by their handsome faces. Most were in their 30s and 40s and exuded health and strength. The difficult prostrations seemed effortless to them.

An hour later, as I attempted to practice meditation on my own, I began to have an even greater appreciation for the discipline required of these men. Sitting cross-legged on a cushion facing the wall of the guesthouse, I struggled to follow the monk Hye Su's teaching. "All can be a Buddha," he said as he paced behind us. "If you awaken to your true nature, you will find happiness. Ponder this."

To be honest, the major thing I found myself pondering was how long we were going to have to wait for breakfast. But even that brief exposure to *chamseon* (meditation) gave me a glimpse into the difficulty of what these monks do for hours each day.

Later that morning, we learned another reason why the monks seemed like they were made of tempered steel. On the lawn before our guesthouse, several monks gave a demonstration of *bulmudo*, a form of martial arts unique to Korean Buddhism. With lightning-fast reflexes the men moved and kicked, suddenly transformed from contemplative monks into ninja-like warriors. Our translator explained that monks in Korea practice martial arts because throughout the nation's history, monasteries have periodically been called upon to defend the nation from invasion. She added that even today monks serve for two years in the South Korean military, as do all Korean males.

Soon it was time to surrender our novice's clothing and pack our bags to leave. But our adventure wasn't over yet. As we prepared to leave the guesthouse, the kindly woman who had spoken to me about the calendar earlier approached me again. While I had seen her from a distance at various times during our time at the monastery, I hadn't had the chance to speak with her at any length. She was obviously pleased to tell me that she had arranged a visit for me with Kwan-Jo, the monk who took the photographs on my calendar. If my husband and I hurried, we could meet with him for a few minutes before our tour bus left the temple.

Grabbing our bags, we followed behind her as she led us to a part of the monastery complex that we hadn't seen before. She knocked on a door, and when a monk answered she whispered to us that we were to do a full-body prostration before him. After we had done so, the monk—a small-statured man who looked to be about seventy years of age—motioned us inside.

Inside the small room, we knelt around a small table and the woman explained that I had been chosen to receive the calendar from the abbot. Then she translated as I thanked him and told him that though I was a Christian, I had learned a great deal from Buddhism. Kwan-Jo nodded, his face expressionless.

Then he did something that seemed to surprise our interpreter as well as my husband and me. Reaching towards a nearby bookshelf, he found a book, opened it, and began writing inside its front cover. Then he handed the book to me.

"It's a book of his photographs," our interpreter said. "He's giving it to you."

The book was clearly expensive, printed on thick paper and containing many hundreds of beautiful photographs. Taken aback by his generosity, I looked first at the interpreter, then at Kwan-Jo. "For me?"

"For you." Both the monk and the woman were now smiling.

"This is beautiful," I said, blinking back tears. "Thank you. Thank you so much."

And then, because we knew the rest of our group was waiting for us, we bowed deeply to the monk and made our goodbyes, with me clutching the two gifts that I had been given, the book and the calendar, as we hurried across the compound.

Before we boarded the tour bus, the woman surprised me yet again by enfolding me in a warm embrace, the sort of goodbye you might give to a sister you know you will not see for a long time.

Turning to my husband, she said, "Make sure you keep her happy for the rest of her life."

As we drove away, we saw her walk back up the hill to the monastery, her figure growing smaller and smaller until finally we could see her no more.

I have thought a great deal about my experiences in the monastery since that day. In one sense the incident with the calendar is a perfect illustration of the difference between two world views. From my Western perspective, I had been chosen at random to receive a symbol of hospitality. From the perspective of the monk and the woman, I was meant to receive two deeply meaningful gifts.

Which world view is correct?

The "real" answer doesn't make any difference, I have come to believe. The deeper truth of my time in the monastery is that in that Buddhist holy place I was greeted with the most radical hospitality that I have ever experienced. I think back to Hye Su telling us that we were all his brothers and sisters, and to the moment when Kwan-Jo handed me the book of his photographs. I remember the warm embrace of the woman as she said goodbye, and her solemn charge to my husband. These were fellow pilgrims who take very seriously the command that they are to honor the Buddha-nature of all the strangers who come to their door.

My experiences make me recall another scene from long ago:

Someone told him, "Your mother and your brothers are standing outside, asking to speak with you." But he said in reply to the one who told him, "Who is my mother? Who are my brothers?" And stretching out his hand toward his disciples, he said, "Here are my mother and my brothers. For whoever does the will of my heavenly Father is my brother, and sister, and mother" (Mt 12:47-50).

To this day, memories of my stay at Beomeosa Temple will return at unexpected times. I remember the sound of the bells tinkling in the breeze and the smell of incense, the flickering of candles in dimly lit halls and the chanting of monks. And I remember that my brothers and sisters are there, linked to me in a way that I cannot rationally explain.

Afterword
Some Final Thoughts on Pilgrimage

A ND now, it's your turn. What places beckon to you? What dream do you want to fulfill? What task does your soul seem to have in store for you? Listen deeply to the small whisper inside of you, the one that will guide you where you need to go.

As you make your plans, keep in mind that it is not necessary to travel great distances while on pilgrimage. No spiritual merit is gained simply by traveling to an exotic location, as the early Irish monk who penned the following verse acknowledges:

> *Who to Rome goes*
> *Much labor, little profit knows;*
> *For God, on earth though long you've sought him,*
> *You'll miss at Rome unless you've brought him.*

Because a pilgrimage is a journey undertaken for a spiritual purpose, its destination can be anywhere, as long as the trip is undertaken mindfully.

Virtually all cultures recognize that there are certain transition points in our lives when we are meant to attend more carefully to matters of the spirit. Adolescents approaching adulthood, seekers arriving at midlife, and those entering the last stage of their lives are all ripe for pilgrimage. So, too, are those who have had a transition thrust upon them unwillingly by death, divorce, or other personal trials. All of these experiences can open our hearts and souls to the new insights to be found on pilgrimage.

I am convinced that the ancient practice of pilgrimage has much to teach the modern world. In our materialistic culture in which travel is often just one more commodity to be consumed, pilgrimage can teach us to slow down, savor the moment, and dive deep into experience. On these transformative journeys, our steps can become acts of devotion to something larger than ourselves, giving us wisdom that will continue to shape our lives once we return home.

As you plan your journey, remember that the call to pilgrimage is in many ways community property. While an ordinary vacation is typically taken as the result of an individual decision, a pilgrim's journey is often intertwined with the lives of other people. You may choose to travel with other seekers, or dedicate your quest to another person's healing or to reconciliation with a long-estranged relative or friend. Wherever you travel, you are likely to bear with you the thoughts and prayers of those you leave behind. These loved ones are your companions on the way, present in your heart even though you may journey alone.

The experience of a friend of mine illustrates how a pilgrimage should be more than just an individualistic enterprise. After much thought and preparation, my friend had undertaken a difficult vision quest in the wilderness, seeking an encounter with something larger than himself. That connection came in the form of an unexpected challenge. After long days of fasting and prayer, my friend heard an immensely ancient and wise voice ask a single question: "On whose behalf do you come?"

The question was deeply troubling to my friend. "I thought I was making the journey on my own behalf, but I had forgotten that a true vision quest is always made on behalf of a tribe," he recalls. "It was both a tremendously powerful and a greatly humbling experience. It made me realize that I lacked a true community, and it sent me back into the world with a resolve to find one."

Those on pilgrimage enter a liminal state, their identities becoming fluid amidst myriad possibilities. That threshold between worlds is sacred ground, and we are meant to honor it with ritual and prayer. Read and reflect before you set out on your trip, preparing your mind and soul for the journey ahead. While you are traveling, intertwine your steps with prayer. Be mindful of each moment. Practice the discipline of gratitude. Look for the grace that can shine through in even the most seemingly mundane of circumstances.

When you return, your re-entry may not be easy. The journey may have changed you in ways that those at home will find hard to understand. Nevertheless, pilgrims are meant to share their new-found wisdom and insights with others. And perhaps more than anything, they are meant to realize that our entire life is meant to be a pilgrimage, a seeking after the divine in moments both ordinary and extraordinary.

Finally, to be a pilgrim is to give up control so that the Holy Spirit can enter into the journey with you. In his book *The Art of Pilgrimage: The Seeker's Guide to Making Travel Sacred*, Phil Cousineau recounts a story about Joseph Campbell, the scholar of ancient myths. A woman approached him after one of his lectures and proceeded to tell him in great detail about her upcoming pilgrimage to Greece. Every last moment had been planned with care, including the exact time of day when she would visit each holy spot. At the end of her long recitation, Campbell took her hand and told her kindly, "Dear lady, I sincerely hope that your trip does not go entirely as planned."

Campbell knew that a true pilgrim must leave room for grace and serendipity along the way. While we may plan the external details of our trip, its larger scope is beyond our control. We do not know the fellow travelers who will change us, the dangers we will face, and the mysteries we will encounter. We must be open to the unexpected, even if it means that we will at times be disappointed, frightened, or confused. To go on pilgrimage is to place ourselves in the hands of God, trusting that the way we need to find will appear before us.

Additional Pilgrimage Sites

El Santuario de Chimayo: Chimayo, New Mexico

Sometimes described as the Lourdes of North America, thousands of pilgrims make their way each year to this simple adobe church in a small village in northern New Mexico. Its fame began around the year 1810, when a local friar saw a light springing from one of the hills near the Santa Cruz River. After following it to its source, he found in the earth a crucifix bearing a dark-skinned Jesus. The local villagers paid homage to the relic and then took it to a church in nearby Santa Cruz. Mysteriously, during the night the crucifix returned to its original location. After this happened two more times, the locals built a small chapel to house the crucifix in Chimayo. Adjacent to the chapel is a small shrine built around the spot where the crucifix was found. Dirt from the floor is given to pilgrims and is said to have healing properties. The most popular time for pilgrimages is Easter week.

Delphi, Greece

The home of the most famous oracle of the ancient Greek world, Delphi is located on a high terrace on the side of Mount Parnassos in Greece. The Greeks believed Delphi to be the center of the earth and the home to the god Apollo. By tradition, the oracle was a woman older than 50 years of age who one day a month would sit near a rock chasm from which strange vapors emerged. The vapors would put her into a trance-like state, during which she would issue prophecies. Today the ruins of Delphi continue to attract pilgrims. Among its most important sites are the Sanctuary of Apollo, the Treasury of the Athenians, and the Castalian Spring, where pilgrims once ritually bathed before entering the sacred precinct.

Anne Frank's House: Amsterdam, Holland

The life of one of the most famous victims of the Holocaust is celebrated in this house in central Amsterdam. For two years during World War II, Anne Frank and seven other people hid in a secret annex of the house to escape capture by the Nazis. In 1944 the group was betrayed and sent to concentration camps. During her time in hiding, the teenage Frank kept a diary that has become one of the world's most widely read books. A visit to the home brings to life the horrors of the Holocaust, but it also celebrates the transcendent spirit of the young Frank. The most precious object in the house is her original diary.

Lisieux, France

This small town in Normandy has become the second-most-visited pilgrimage site in France (after Lourdes) because of its connection to St. Therese, the Little Flower of Jesus. Born Therese Martin, Therese came to Lisieux as a young girl in 1877. Ten years later she entered the local Carmelite convent, where she died of tuberculosis at the age of 24. Virtually unknown at her death, Therese left behind a memoir, *Story of a Soul,* that has been translated into more than fifty languages. Named a Doctor of the Church in 1997, St. Therese is one of the world's most popular saints. In Lisieux pilgrims can visit the Basilica of St. Therese, her childhood home, and the Carmelite convent where her body lies.

Vatican City, Rome

Steeped in Christian tradition and history, Rome is one of the most-visited pilgrimage sites in the world. Vatican City is the 109-acre walled enclave within Rome that is the seat of the papacy. Its centerpiece is St. Peter's Basilica, built over the site where the body of St. Peter is said to be buried. In front of the basilica lies St. Peter's Square, designed by the artist Bernini in the seventeenth century. Vatican City is full of artistic as well as religious treasures, including the ceiling frescos of the Sistine Chapel and the *Pieta,* both by Michelangelo. The Vatican Museums are the finest in the world, containing thousands of artistic masterpieces spanning many centuries.

Jerusalem, Israel

The capital of Israel attracts pilgrims from three faiths: Judaism, Christianity, and Islam. For Jews, the holiest site is the Western Wall, which is the only remaining remnant of the Second Temple. Among the sites revered by Christians are the Church of the Holy Sepulchre (where Jesus is believed to have been buried and resurrected), the Mount of Olives (where Jesus prayed during the night of his betrayal), and the Via Dolorosa (which tradition says is the route taken by Jesus to the cross). Muslims make pilgrimages to the Dome of the Rock, one of their holiest shrines. Another deeply moving site is Yad Vashem, the museum that serves as a memorial to the six million victims of the Holocaust.

Basilica de Guadalupe: Mexico City, Mexico

The most visited shrine in North America is located in Mexico City. It is dedicated to the Virgin of Guadalupe, who appeared to the Indian peasant Juan Diego in 1531 and told him that she wished to have a church built in her honor. Her image was later miraculously imprinted upon his tunic. Two basilicas stand at the shrine today. One was built in the eighteenth century; the other constructed in the 1970s. Inside the latter structure is Diego's tunic, an object of veneration for pilgrims. The Virgin of Guadalupe's feast day is December 12, when many thousands of people journey to the shrine.

Mt. Sinai and St. Catherine's Monastery: Sinai Desert, Egypt

Mt. Sinai (known locally as Gebel Musa) is believed to be the site where Moses received the Ten Commandments. For thousands of years pilgrims have climbed to its summit, usually starting in the pre-dawn hours so that they can view the sunrise from its top. At the base of the mountain, St. Catherine's Monastery is home to a community of Greek Orthodox monks. Built in the sixth century, St. Catherine's is one of the oldest monasteries in the world and is home to a priceless collection of icons, paintings, mosaics, altar pieces, and illuminated manuscripts.

Glastonbury, England

This site in southwest England is shrouded in myth and legend. Glastonbury Tor, the tallest hill in the region, was likely a site for pre-Christian worship. Among the many legends associated with Glastonbury is one that says that after Jesus' crucifixion, Joseph of Arimathea took the cup used at the Last Supper and brought it here, where it became the Holy Grail of Arthurian legend. The body of King Arthur is said to lie underneath the ruins of the abbey.

Abbey of Gethsemani: Trappist, Kentucky

Pilgrims who treasure the writings of Thomas Merton find inspiration in this monastery in rural Kentucky. Merton entered the monastic community at the abbey in 1941 and lived here until his death in 1968. A prolific writer, Merton's works include his autobiography, *The Seven Storey Mountain,* as well spiritual classics such as

New Seeds of Contemplation. The abbey is home to sixty-five monks, who welcome pilgrims for retreats. Guests may join the monks in keeping the liturgy of the hours and attend Eucharist.

Additional Titles Published by Resurrection Press, a Catholic Book Publishing Imprint

A Rachel Rosary *Larry Kupferman*	$4.50
Blessings All Around *Dolores Leckey*	$8.95
Catholic Is Wonderful *Mitch Finley*	$4.95
Discernment *Chris Aridas*	$8.95
Edge of Greatness *Joni Woelfel*	$9.95
Growing through the Stress of Ministry *Muto/van Kaam*	$7.95
Grace Notes *Lorraine Murray*	$9.95
Healing through the Mass *Robert DeGrandis, SSJ*	$9.95
Our Grounds for Hope *Fulton J. Sheen*	$7.95
The Healing Rosary *Mike D.*	$5.95
Healing the Wounds of Emotional Abuse *Nancy deFlon*	$6.95
Heart Peace *Adolfo Quezada*	$9.95
Hold Fast to Hope *Linda Rooney*	$6.95
Life, Love and Laughter *Jim Vlaun*	$7.95
The Joy of Being an Altar Server *Joseph Champlin*	$5.95
The Joy of Being a Bereavement Minister *Nancy Stout*	$5.95
The Joy of Being a Catechist *Gloria Durka*	$4.95
The Joy of Being a Eucharistic Minister *Mitch Finley*	$5.95
The Joy of Being a Lector *Mitch Finley*	$5.95
The Joy of Being an Usher *Gretchen Hailer, RSHM*	$5.95
The Joy of Marriage Preparation *McDonough/Marinelli*	$5.95
The Joy of Music Ministry *J.M. Talbot*	$6.95
The Joy of Praying the Rosary *James McNamara*	$5.95
The Joy of Teaching *Joanmarie Smith*	$5.95
Lessons for Living from the 23rd Psalm *Victor M. Parachin*	$6.95
Lights in the Darkness *Ave Clark, O.P.*	$8.95
Loving Yourself for God's Sake *Adolfo Quezada*	$5.95
Magnetized by God *Robert E. Lauder*	$8.95
Mercy Flows *Rod Damico*	$9.95
Mother Teresa *Eugene Palumbo, S.D.B.*	$5.95
Mourning Sickness *Keith Smith*	$8.95
The Power of One *Jim Lisante*	$9.95
Praying the Lord's Prayer with Mary *Muto/vanKaam*	$8.95
5-Minute Miracles *Linda Schubert*	$4.95
Sabbath Moments *Adolfo Quezada*	$6.95
Season of New Beginnings *Mitch Finley*	$4.95
Sometimes I Haven't Got a Prayer *Mary Sherry*	$8.95
The Spiritual Spa *Mary Sherry*	$9.95
St. Katharine Drexel *Daniel McSheffery*	$12.95
What He Did for Love *Francis X. Gaeta*	$5.95
Woman Soul *Pat Duffy, OP*	$7.95
You Are My Beloved *Mitch Finley*	$10.95

For a free catalog call 1-800-892-6657
www.catholicbookpublishing.com